Northern Right Whale

Fin Whale

Fin Whale – *right side of jaw*

Sei Whale

Minke Whale

Cuvier's Beaked Whale

Northern Bottle-nosed Whale

SCALE
metres
0 1 2 3 4

OCEAN *Guides*

Whales & Dolphins
of the
European Atlantic
The English Channel and the Bay of Biscay

Graeme Cresswell
Dylan Walker

Artwork by Rob Still & Phil Coles

WILD*Guides*

First published 2001 by **WILD**_Guides_ Ltd.

WILD_Guides_ Ltd.
Parr House
63 Hatch Lane
Old Basing
Hampshire
RG24 7EB

www.wildguides.co.uk

ISBN 1-903657-00-8

© 2001 Graeme Cresswell and Dylan Walker,
       Rob Still (digital artwork, maps and colour illustrations)
       Phil Coles (black and white illustrations)

       Edited by Andy Swash

Production and design by **WILD**_Guides_ Ltd, Old Basing, Hampshire.
Printed in China. The Hanway Press Ltd, London.

CONTENTS

Foreword

Since whale and dolphin watching began in earnest in North America in the early 1970s, the opportunity to experience the thrill of close encounters with cetaceans has led to a tremendous increase in demand from the public. Today, whale-watching is a significant leisure industry along the east and west coasts of the USA, Canada, the coast of Iceland and in many other parts of the world. Operators currently take thousands of people a year on trips to see inquisitive gray whales, lunge-feeding humpback whales, hunting orcas and bow-riding dolphins.

European waters have, until recently, been considered by most people to be comparatively impoverished in terms of the potential for whale and dolphin watching. However, studies during the 1990s by volunteer researchers, including the authors of this book, have helped to confirm that the waters of the north-eastern Atlantic are inhabited by over a quarter of the all of the world's known species of whales, dolphins and porpoises. Furthermore, these studies suggest that the region supports a significant proportion of the world population of a number of these species.

In the light of these and other findings, there has been a recent increase in interest in these animals and also the number of commercial whale-watching destinations and the volume of research being carried out in European and adjacent waters. As illustrated by this book, properly regulated whale-watching can contribute profoundly to education and cetacean research.

It is now possible to watch cetaceans throughout the Atlantic waters of Europe and Scandinavia, including blue whales feeding off Iceland, bottle-nosed dolphins playing close to shore around the UK, inquisitive short-finned pilot whales close to the major tourist destinations of the Canary Islands, and sperm whales and other species in the Azores.

The production of this book, the first of its kind to cover the cetaceans of European waters, is therefore very timely. It is essential reading for anyone with an interest in finding, identifying and learning more about the whales and dolphins of the region, providing, as it does, a comprehensive guide to all the species recorded. The book illustrates how cetaceans appear at the sea surface and provides the most recent information on how best to identify them from land or at sea. This compact book is simple to use and clearly presented, the text is concise, and the innovative use of digital technology has produced a remarkable collection of plates.

The Whale and Dolphin Conservation Society wholeheartedly recommends this book to all cetacean enthusiasts, and is delighted at the publisher's generous commitment to make a donation to cetacean conservation for every copy sold. By buying and reading this book, and by watching and understanding more about cetaceans, everyone can help to safeguard the future of these fantastic animals.

Chris Stroud
Chief Executive
Whale and Dolphin Conservation Society

WDCS
Whale and Dolphin Conservation Society

Introduction

This is the first comprehensive guide to the identification of whales, dolphins and porpoises (collectively known as cetaceans) in the European Atlantic. Until very recently, most researchers and whale-watchers were unaware of the great variety of cetaceans that can be seen so close to the shores of western Europe. Indeed, it is only during the last decade, when detailed cetacean surveys have been carried out in earnest, that we have discovered how important this area is for cetacean biodiversity.

This field guide describes all of the 27 species of whale, dolphin and porpoise that have occurred in the European Atlantic. Knowledge of the identification of cetaceans at sea is developing rapidly and this book aims to provide an easy-to-use, detailed guide for both the ocean-going and land-based whale-watcher. For every species there is a description of the key identification features, notes on how to separate it from similar species, a brief natural history, and a map showing its known distribution and likelihood of occurrence. Facing each species account is a colour plate which has been created, using the latest digital image technology, from up to four separate surface photographs. These photographs have been carefully selected to illustrate the key identification features. Whilst photographs of cetaceans at sea usually only reveal a part of the animal, be it the back, the dorsal fin, a raised tail or merely a blow, such images are considered to be the most informative way of aiding identification, since they show the animal from the whale-watcher's perspective.

Because whales and dolphins often only show a small proportion of their bodies at the surface, and may only be seen briefly, observers have in the past often considered definite identification to be too difficult. Although some species are rarely seen at sea, either because they avoid boats, live far from shore or remain submerged for long periods of time, and their identification is still poorly known, in most cases identifying cetaceans at sea is not always as difficult as it may first appear. There are many features to look for and, with experience, it is often easy to identify a whale or dolphin at a considerable distance. Whilst little is known of the biology and identification of some species within the European Atlantic, our understanding of these mysterious animals is increasing all the time. For example, this is the first publication ever to show photographs taken at sea of the four species of Mesoplodon beaked whale currently known to occur in the North Atlantic. These photographs have provided some new pointers to the identification of this particularly difficult group.

It is hoped that this guide will encourage more whale-watchers to explore the waters of the European Atlantic, thereby adding to our knowledge on the status and distribution of these wonderful animals. If you have any photographs of any of the species described in this book, or of other cetaceans from further afield which might be suitable for inclusion in future **OCEAN** *Guides* publications, please email the authors: photos@wildguides.co.uk.

Acknowledgements

The authors would like to say a special thank you to the following people. To all the volunteers who have conducted whale and dolphin surveys in the English Channel and Bay of Biscay since 1995, without whom this book would not have been possible.

To the Captain and crew of both ferry companies for their assistance, and to the ORCA committee who have worked so hard to raise the profile of cetaceans in the European Atlantic. Particular thanks are also due to Lisa Gorman for her assistance and support; to Andy Swash for his excellent editing skills; to Steve Holmes for his valuable comments and to Phil Coles for producing such first class illustrations at very short notice. We are very grateful to Catherine Baron and Cris Sellares for their respective French and Spanish translations and advice on species' names; and to Judith Vandrak for inspiration.

Thank you to all of the photographers for their help and patience. Last but certainly not least, a special thank you to Rob Still, our publisher and artist, for his enthusiasm, imaginative ideas and work rate, all of which have helped to make this project all the more rewarding.

The European Atlantic

For the purposes of this book, the European Atlantic is divided into four regions based on their differing topography. When discussing the distribution of cetacean species, these regions will be referred to regularly (*see map below and on page 49*). From north to south they are: the English Channel, the Brittany Coast, and the northern and southern parts of the Bay of Biscay (the Northern Bay and Southern Bay respectively).

English Channel

The English Channel between the south coast of England and 48°40'N is an area of shallow water at a depth generally less than 100 m. Although it has received considerable coverage during cetacean surveys, sightings are generally scarce in comparison with the other regions.

Brittany Coast

The Brittany Coast lies between 48°40'N and the 200 m depth contour at a latitude of approximately 46°20'N. This is also a shallow water area over the continental shelf, with water depth averaging between 100–150 m.

Northern Bay

The Northern Bay lies between the 200 m depth contour in the north and 44°30'N in the south. The steep topography of the shelf-edge here results in a sharp increase in water depth from 200 m to 4,000 m, before levelling at around the 4,000 m mark. Beyond this lies the abyssal plain of the ocean floor.

Southern Bay

The Southern Bay covers an area from 44°30'N, southward to the north coast of Spain. This is an area with a tremendous variation in depth, with two extensive deep-water canyons that fall beneath the transect lines of the two ferries which ply between south-west England and northern Spain. These are the Torrelavaga Canyon on the Brittany Ferries route and the Santander Canyon on the P&O European Ferries route. The southern Bay also encompasses a small area of continental shelf.

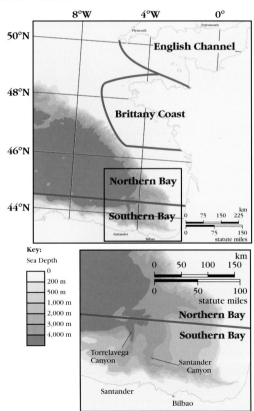

What is a cetacean?

All whales, dolphins and porpoises belong to an Order of marine mammals called Cetacea, and are collectively known as cetaceans. Like other mammals, cetaceans are warm-blooded, breathe air through their lungs and suckle their young. However, unlike most other mammals, cetaceans live exclusively in water. Their adaptations for life in the oceans are so advanced that many cetaceans superficially resemble fish, particularly sharks, in form and structure. One of the best ways of differentiating a cetacean from a fish is by looking at the orientation of the tail: horizontal in cetaceans, vertical in fish.

There are approximately 80 species within the Order Cetacea. These are divided into two groups or Sub-orders: the Mysticeti or baleen whales, and the Odontoceti or toothed whales.
• Baleen whales range in size from the Pygmy Right Whale, which barely reaches 7 m in length, to the massive Blue Whale, which grows to over 30 m. Instead of teeth, these whales have plates of baleen (whalebone) which hang from the roof of their mouths. These vertical plates can grow to over 2 m in length in some species and are used to filter enormous quantities of small fish and crustaceans. Baleen whales have two external nostrils or blow-holes.
• Toothed whales range in size from the huge Sperm Whale, with a maximum length of 18 m, to the diminutive Harbour Porpoise, which reaches a maximum length of 1·8 m. Besides having teeth, the Odontoceti are distinguished by having only one external nostril or blow-hole. Nearly 70 species of toothed whale are recognised, the smallest of which are generally known as dolphins or porpoises.

The following diagrams illustrate the main differences between the baleen and toothed whales, and give the names of the key external body parts which can be important in identification.

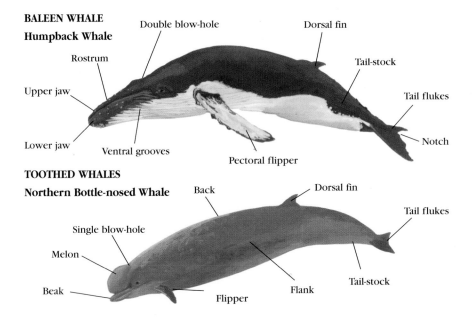

BALEEN WHALE
Humpback Whale

Double blow-hole · Dorsal fin · Rostrum · Tail-stock · Upper jaw · Tail flukes · Lower jaw · Notch · Ventral grooves · Pectoral flipper

TOOTHED WHALES
Northern Bottle-nosed Whale

Back · Dorsal fin · Tail flukes · Single blow-hole · Melon · Beak · Flipper · Flank · Tail-stock

Finding cetaceans

When

Whales, dolphins and porpoises must return to the surface to breathe on a regular basis, so can be seen at any time of day. The amount of time spent at the surface varies greatly from species to species and is also dependent upon whether the animal is resting, feeding or travelling. However, perhaps the most important factor in terms of when to watch whales is the season. Different species occur in different waters in different months, so the dedicated whale-watcher is likely to encounter a greater diversity of cetaceans by watching in all seasons. However, it is widely accepted that in temperate regions of the world, such as the European Atlantic, summer, and particularly late summer, is the best whale-watching period. There are several reasons for this: the weather, and therefore the sea, is generally at its calmest; high-pressure weather systems often settle for considerable periods bringing warm, sunny and windless conditions; and day length is at its greatest – allowing more hours for whale-watching during a voyage.

These factors combine to increase water temperature as summer progresses, allowing phytoplankton (the 'green grass' of the marine ecosystem) to flourish. At this time of year, these free-floating marine plants increase in numbers dramatically, providing food, either directly or indirectly, for all marine creatures ranging from microscopic zooplankton to 100 tonne whales. This great abundance of food is often concentrated in certain areas, particularly where ocean currents rich in nutrients are forced to the surface. It is in such areas that whales and dolphins often congregate and it is therefore unsurprising that the peak months for whale-watching in the European Atlantic are from July to September.

Where

Most cetaceans, like their mammalian relatives on land, are at the top of the food-chain. Such predators tend to be sparsely distributed and difficult to find, so knowing where to look is very important.

Some cetaceans favour shallow waters or coastal areas, whereas others prefer the shelf slope, or restrict themselves to very deep water. Some are resident, whilst others are migratory. With experience, and the aid of marine charts and global positioning systems, the whale-watcher will become increasingly familiar with habitat preferences which can help with identification. For example, Minke and Northern Bottle-nosed Whales look almost identical when only the upper back and dorsal fin is seen, but Minke Whales generally occur over the shelf, often close to shore, whereas Northern Bottle-nosed Whales are more likely to be encountered in deep offshore waters.

Whilst water depth and sea floor topography can be useful indicators of the presence of a particular species, this alone should never be used as a way of identifying a cetacean specifically. Part of the joy of watching whales and dolphins is their complete unpredictability. It is almost impossible to guess where they will be because they can pop up anywhere at any time. Some European dolphins have even been recorded over 100 km up river! Whales and dolphins do not follow any rules. They roam freely over great distances and there is still much to learn about their distribution and migratory patterns.

For the dedicated whale-watcher, the most important principle is to put in as much effort as possible. The longer you watch, the better your chances are of seeing something. It is as simple as that!

How

When searching for cetaceans, it is very important to choose a good place from which to watch. On land, the best locations are headlands with a reasonably high vantage point, particularly those which extend to deeper water. Binoculars and often a telescope are useful tools for land-based watching. If you are watching from a boat, you should always carry binoculars. The bridge or close to the bow are good places from which to search, since this allows the observer to look forward and beyond the bow. A stable platform helps the observer to use binoculars without too much shake. Elevation is also an important consideration, particularly in rougher seas when a high vantage-point allows the observer to track cetaceans as they travel through wave troughs. Other important factors include sheltering from the wind, and avoiding glare from the sun and sea spray.

Finding cetaceans can require a great deal of patience. Keep searching over the same area of water even if you think there is nothing there. Some cetaceans can stay under water for an hour or more before eventually surfacing, and even when animals remain at the surface it is surprising how easy they are to miss. A 15 m long Sperm Whale can easily be overlooked when it lies motionless at the surface with only a small proportion of its upper back showing.

Cetacean watching is generally easiest in relatively calm weather. A sea state of three or less, when there are few or no white caps to the waves, is preferable (*see Weather, below*). In these conditions, large whales and leaping dolphins are often first noticed by the white water they create as they surface. The breath or 'blow' is another feature that can help to locate a large whale. Blows can often be seen several kilometres away and last for several seconds. Having observed an unusual splash or a possible blow, check with binoculars. It may be nothing, but more often than not, your first impressions will be correct and you will have found a cetacean!

Weather

Weather conditions in the Bay of Biscay and English Channel relate closely to those of southern England and western France. Winter generally sees a series of wet and windy fronts pushing north-east across the North Atlantic, creating choppy to stormy conditions for long periods. As spring approaches, the weather improves and by mid-summer sunny days and calm seas predominate. In July, August and early September these conditions can last for weeks, and are perfect for whale-watching. From mid-September the weather starts to become more unpredictable, worsening slightly as autumn turns to winter.

The Sun's glare, fog, sea swell, rain and wind can all affect the chances of locating whales and dolphins, but by far the most important factor is the sea state. Sea state is the term used to describe the wave formation created by the wind. A sea state of three or less, when the waves have few or no white caps, is generally considered to be most conducive to whale-watching and cetacean surveying. Anything higher and it is certainly easy to miss at least the diminutive Harbour Porpoise.

Sea state can be measured using the following guide:

0	Mirror calm; whale-watching heaven!
1	Slight ripples; no white water
2	Small wavelets; glassy crests, no white caps
3	Large wavelets; crests begin to break; few white caps
4	Longer waves; many white caps; whale-watching becomes more tricky
5	Moderate waves of longer form; some spray
6	Large waves; many white caps; frequent spray
7	Sea heaps up; white foam blows in streaks
8	Long, high waves; edges breaking; foam blows in streaks
9	High waves; sea begins to roll; dense foam streaks; scary!

Identifying cetaceans

Sightings of cetaceans are often brief, and it is therefore important to concentrate on key features to help with identification. In approximate order of importance, these are:

1. SIZE   Due to the relatively uniform nature of the surface of the sea, judging the size of a cetacean can be extremely difficult. Try to compare the size of the cetacean with other familiar objects at a similar distance, such as fishing boats or seabirds. When observing a cetacean, remember that often only a small portion of the animal will be visible above the surface at any one time. For example, a Blue Whale rolling at the surface will often show less of its body than does the smaller Fin Whale, giving a misleading impression that the former is the smaller animal.

2. SHAPE   Cetaceans come in many shapes, ranging from long and slim, through rotund and bulky, to short and sleek. It is, therefore, very important to try to judge the shape of an animal.

3. DORSAL FIN   The size, shape and position of the dorsal fin is a very useful aid to identification, particularly in whales. Apart from the extremely rare Northern Right Whale, all cetacean species occurring in the European Atlantic show a dorsal fin. The shape of this fin varies greatly and can be triangular, sickle-shaped or merely a hump. In some species, there is often a considerable variation in fin shape and size between individuals. Try to determine the size of the fin in relation to the length of the body, its position along the back and, in large whales, its appearance at the surface in relation to the blow-hole.

4. BLOW   In many of the large cetaceans, a tall jet of water is expelled as the animal surfaces and breathes out. This is known as the blow, the size and shape of which varies between species and with the activity of the individual. Blows can be a helpful clue to identification in combination with other features. However, because they are so variable and may be affected by the wind, they should never be used in isolation to identify a whale to specific level.

5. COLORATION AND PATTERNING   The colour of a cetacean can be very difficult to judge. Since the sea itself often looks very different on the port (left) and starboard (right) sides of a ship due to the position of the sun, the observer may be reduced to using the terms light and dark to describe a cetacean. However, coloration and patterning are key features in the identification of some cetaceans, particularly members of the dolphin family which can otherwise appear very similar.

6. BEHAVIOUR   Most cetaceans are highly social animals and exhibit a variety of interesting and distinct behaviours, some of which are depicted below. Cetacean behaviour can sometimes be used to aid identification. For example, some large whales such as Blue, Humpback and Sperm Whales, regularly raise their tails on diving (fluking), unlike Fin, Sei and Minke Whales.

Examples of cetacean behaviour

Chorus line - *travelling in a line abreast*

Tail-slapping - *splashing tail on surface*

Blow - *water expelled vertically during exhalation*

Fluking - *raising tail flukes before a dive*

Logging - *lying motionless at the surface*

Spy-hopping - *head is lifted and held out of the water*

Breaching - *lifting body out of water and splashing down on the surface*

Porpoising - *raising part or all of the body clear of the water whilst travelling*

Whale-watching from ferries

Two ferry services run from the south coast of England to the north coast of Spain, offering excellent opportunities for whale-watching. P&O Portsmouth ferries operate between Portsmouth and Bilbao, whilst Brittany Ferries ply the waters between Plymouth and Santander. Both sail in all seasons and their routes cover all four regions of the European Atlantic (*see The European Atlantic, Page 6*). The upper deck on both vessels is generally the best place from which to look. On the Brittany ferry it is possible to look forward and beyond the bow, allowing animals to be located and tracked ahead of the boat. Unfortunately, this is not possible onboard the P&O ferry, where two or more observers are required to take part in any watch in order to cover both the port and starboard sides. Although the bridge of the P&O ferry obscures the view of the bow, it does protect the deck from any head-wind, making it easier to use binoculars.

The ferries travel at around 15–17 knots (nautical miles per hour), allowing cetaceans to be seen for a reasonable length of time. Sightings generally last from a few seconds to a few minutes, but if animals are seen ahead of the ship it may be possible to observe them for as long as 20 minutes.

Both ferries are amongst the largest in Europe and the viewing platforms are about 30 m above sea level. When first on board this seems ridiculously high and it is easy to imagine that you will not see anything. Fortunately, cetaceans are quite large animals and this high vantage point often allows the observer to look down through the clear water to see whales and dolphins swimming below the surface. It is also a distinct advantage when sea swell increases, as cetaceans are easily lost behind the waves at lower angles. The height of the platform also makes it easy to see the formation and spacing of whole pods of dolphins and whales as they hunt, travel or rest at the surface. This is usually difficult to do from a small boat.

The other great advantage of whale-watching from such a large vessel is its stability. Large ships are so stable that in relatively calm conditions it is possible to use a tripod-mounted telescope and identify cetaceans at a considerable distance. Perhaps just as important to the discerning whale-watcher is the element of additional comfort provided – something which would certainly be lacking on a smaller vessel. Luxuries come in the form of jacuzzis, swimming pools, cinemas, beauty therapists, value-for-money shopping and good restaurants. If you do choose to dine during daylight hours, be sure to grab a window seat as many passengers have added the likes of Fin Whale, Cuvier's Beaked Whale and Striped Dolphin to the à la carte menu!

On a calm day, it is possible to watch cetaceans through a telescope from the deck.

Cetacean families

The cetaceans recorded in the European Atlantic can be divided into seven groups (which are broadly equivalent to Families). This section aims to provide a brief overview of the key features which identify these groups, a broad knowledge of which is an essential first step towards identifying the different species at sea. It also provides certain historical background information.

RIGHT and BOWHEAD WHALES   Family: Baleanidae

Northern Right Whale

Northern Right Whale (Plate 1)

This Family comprises some of the largest whales in the world. Three species are known: two right whales and the Bowhead Whale. Like the rorquals (Balaenopteridae), right and Bowhead Whales are very heavy, have a distinctive tall blow, and capture vast amounts of prey by filter-feeding. However, they differ from the rorquals in several respects. The body is much more stocky, with a broad back, completely lacking a dorsal fin. The head is huge, up to a quarter of the overall body length. The mouth consists of massive arched lips, within which lie very long baleen plates. Unlike the rorquals, the throat cannot be extended to take in more water but the baleen plates help to overcome this disadvantage by increasing the whale's filtering capacity. All three species are highly specialised plankton feeders.

The Northern Right Whale is the only member of the Baleanidae to occur in the European Atlantic. This was one of the first species to be hunted by early whalers as it frequently came close to shore, did not shy away from boats and floated when killed. It soon became known as the 'right whale to catch', hence its present-day name. Hunting along the Biscay coast began around 1000 AD, and had spread across the ocean to Newfoundland by 1500 AD, continuing into the 20th century. Historically, the estimated population was 10,000–50,000 individuals but, although protected since 1949, this whale remains close to extinction. Less than 350 animals survive today, most occurring between Newfoundland and Florida.

RORQUAL WHALES   Family: Baleanopteridae

Blue Whale

Blue Whale (Plate 1)
Sei Whale (Plate 2)
Fin Whale (Plate 2)
Humpback Whale (Plate 3)
Minke Whale (Plate 3)

With the exception of the Minke Whale, all rorqual whales are large to very large. They include the Blue Whale, the biggest animal ever to have lived on this planet. Sadly, rorquals formed the mainstay of the whaling industry during the 19th and 20th centuries, pushing several species to the brink of extinction. Following the international ban on whaling in 1986, some stocks have shown signs of a slow recovery, but many populations remain severely depleted.

Rorquals have several features which distinguish them from the other groups. The name rorqual is derived from the Norwegian word '*rorvhal*' which refers to the series of throat grooves that extend underneath the lower jaw. Rorquals do not possess teeth, instead having a series of comb-like structures called baleen plates which hang from the upper jaw. They feed by opening their cavernous jaws as they swim along, and expanding their throat grooves, vastly increasing the volume of water held within. When the mouth is finally closed, water is strained through the baleen plates leaving quantities of small fish and zooplankton trapped inside.

Despite their enormous size, rorquals are streamlined and capable of considerable speed. They have large, flattened heads with a centrally-located twin blow-hole. The larger species can exhale a vertical blow several metres high. Most members of this group migrate long distances between their cold water summer feeding grounds and warm water winter breeding grounds. Six species of rorqual are known, five of which occur in the European Atlantic.

SPERM WHALES   Families: Kogidae and Physeteridae

Sperm Whale

Pygmy Sperm Whale (Plate 4)
Dwarf Sperm Whale (Plate 4)
Sperm Whale (Plate 5)

Although sperm whales include the largest and the smallest toothed whales from two different families, their basic body shapes are quite similar. Sperm whales are characterised by their bulky body, large, squarish head and narrow, underslung lower jaw lined with teeth. The single blow-hole is positioned slightly to the left of the top of the head producing a blow which is angled forward and to the left when the whale exhales.

All known species of sperm whale have been recorded in the European Atlantic.

BEAKED WHALES   Family: Ziphiidae

Northern Bottle-nosed Whale

Northern Bottle-nosed Whale (Plate 6)
Cuvier's Beaked Whale (Plate 6)
Sowerby's Beaked Whale (Plate 7)
Blainville's Beaked Whale (Plate 7)
True's Beaked Whale (Plate 8)
Gervais' Beaked Whale (Plate 8)

These medium-sized whales are unique in possessing a distinctive protruding jaw, or beak. The forehead is often bulbous, the body relatively stream-lined (often showing scarring) and the dorsal fin is smallish, located two-thirds of the way towards the tail. The centre of the trailing edge of the tail has no notch.

Due to their similar body shapes and coloration, most beaked whales, particularly those in the genus *Mesoplodon* (Plates 7 & 8), are notoriously difficult to identify. The main difference between the species in this genus is the position of protruding teeth which erupt only in mature males. The observer will almost certainly have to note, and ideally photograph, this feature to prove identification.

Six of the 20 species of beaked whale known occur in the European Atlantic. However, because of their deep-water habits and unobtrusive behaviour almost nothing is known about any of them. Beaked whales are capable of diving for considerable periods of time, and to great depths, in search of their squid and deep-sea fish prey. Two new species of beaked whale have been discovered in the last decade, indicative of the enormous amount still to be learnt about the distribution, ecology and identification of this mysterious family.

BLACKFISH   Family: Delphinidae

Short-finned Pilot Whale

Long-finned Pilot Whale (Plate 12)
Short-finned Pilot Whale (Plate 12)
False Killer Whale (Plate 13)
Orca or *Killer Whale* (Plate 13)

Blackfish include the largest members of the dolphin family, but each species is named as a whale because it attains a similar size to the beaked and other medium-sized whales. As the name suggests, they are predominantly black in colour. The dorsal fin is relatively large and prominent. A low, bushy blow can usually be seen emanating from the single blow-hole on surfacing. The jaws are rounded, containing many well-developed conical teeth, and the beak is small or lacking. Like other dolphins, blackfish are highly social animals, often living their entire lives in discrete family groups. They are efficient, pack-hunting predators, capable of considerable speed and exhibit a range of interesting behaviour such as spy-hopping, tail-slapping and breaching. They prey on a great variety of fish, squid and other sea life, including marine mammals. Four of the six species of blackfish occur in the European Atlantic.

DOLPHINS   Family: Delphinidae

Common Dolphin

Rough-toothed Dolphin (Plate 9)
Bottle-nosed Dolphin (Plate 9)
Common Dolphin (Plate 10)
Striped Dolphin (Plate 10)
Atlantic White-sided Dolphin (Plate 11)
White-beaked Dolphin (Plate 11)
Risso's Dolphin (Plate 14)

Dolphins are smaller than most whale species, have slim, streamlined bodies and, in most cases, tall, prominent and centrally-placed dorsal fins. Their bodies show a variety of patterns and colours which are often key to their identification. The heads of most species taper gently to a prominent beak which contains many sharp teeth. They are generally social animals, often occuring in large groups and are capable of great speed and spectacular acrobatics. They prey upon a wide variety of squid, fish and other marine life. Seven of the 31 known species of dolphin occur in the European Atlantic.

PORPOISES   **Family: Phocoenidae**

Harbour Porpoise (Plate 14)

Porpoises are the smallest of all cetaceans, reaching 1·2–2·0 m. They do not have a prominent beak and the body, though streamlined, is quite robust. Most species are timid, rarely performing the kinds of acrobatics commonly associated with dolphins. They frequent inshore waters, feeding mostly on small fish. Unfortunately, the pressures on many coastal populations through over-fishing, accidental capture in fishing nets, and pollution have caused significant declines in several species to the extent that they are currently considered threatened. Of the six known species of porpoise, only one occurs in the European Atlantic.

Harbour Porpoise

Minke Whale breaching

How to use this guide

Each species of cetacean recorded in the European Atlantic is depicted in the following plates. The accompanying text follows a consistent format, as outlined below:

English Name *Scientific name*   F: French name
                                                        ESP: Spanish name

Illustration of the species indicating the proportion of the animal typically observed above the surface. The two species on each page are shown to the same scale.

Adult length: 11–18m
Group size: 1–3, sometimes more
Breaching: Often, sometimes repeatedly
Deep Dive: Usually raises tail flukes
Blow: Distinctive, high, V-shaped blow when viewed from front

Box indicating 'at-a-glance' the size, typical group size, key behavioural features and nature of blow (if appropriate) of each species.

IDENTIFICATION: A concise description of the species, detailing the key identification features to look for.
SIMILAR SPECIES: Highlights the differences between confusion species.
BEHAVIOUR: Summarises the key aspects of the behaviour of the species, covering group behaviour, feeding strategies and swimming action.
STATUS AND DISTRIBUTION: Outlines the distribution of the species both in the region and in a global context.

Map showing the distribution of the species within the European Atlantic.

The species distribution maps in this book are intended as a general guide only. It is important to note that the distribution of many species is poorly known, due to the relatively small number of recorded sightings at sea and the fact that large areas of the region have rarely, if ever, been surveyed.

KEY
⬛ Regularly seen
☐ Sometimes seen
☐ Rarely observed

Bar chart
J F M A M J J A S O N D
Relative abundance of the species in each month. A red dot indicates a stranding. A "?" indicates a possible sighting.

Full details of each photograph featured in the book are given in the photographic and artwork credits section on page 54. This includes a description of the image and, where known, details of where and when the photograph was taken and by whom. The photographs are listed in the order in which they appear on the plate, from top to bottom.

PLATE 1

Northern Right Whale *Eubalaena glacialis*

F: Baleine franche boréale
ESP: Ballena franca

Adult length: 11–18m
Group size: 1–3, sometimes more
Breaching: Often, sometimes repeatedly
Deep Dive: Usually raises tail flukes
Blow: Distinctive, high, V-shaped blow when viewed from front

IDENTIFICATION: The Northern Right Whale is strikingly different from the other large whales of the European Atlantic. The first clue to its presence is usually the distinctive blow which is V-shaped when viewed from the front or rear of the whale. The body is large and bulky and there is no dorsal fin, only a broad, flat and very dark back which often remains quite low in the water. The huge head has light-coloured lumps (callosities), particularly around the rostrum and blow-holes, above the eyes, and along the lower jaw. Callosities are hardened patches of skin which become pale due to infestations of whale lice. The tail flukes, which are often raised on sounding, are very large and all black, with smooth edges, pointed tips and a deep central notch.

SIMILAR SPECIES: The V-shaped blow, large, flat back lacking a dorsal fin and characteristic callosities on the top of the head are diagnostic. Confusion is possible with other large whales which have deceptively variable blows and may sometimes surface so that their dorsal fin remains below the surface.

BEHAVIOUR: Northern Right Whales are slow swimmers and are inquisitive and approachable. They can exhibit a range of behaviours such as lob-tailing, flipper-waving and breaching, sometimes up to ten times in a row, landing with a resounding splash that can be heard up to a distance of 1 km.

STATUS AND DISTRIBUTION: In the North Atlantic, these whales spend the summer feeding in temperate and boreal waters as far north as Newfoundland, Iceland and Norway. During this time they subsist almost entirely on tiny copepods. In winter, the whales return to breed in temperate to sub-tropical waters as far south as Florida and sub-Saharan Africa. This species was once abundant in the Bay of Biscay, and early taxonomists named it *Eubalaena biscayensis*. Sadly, it is almost extinct in the European Atlantic today and there has been only one recent sighting despite intensive surveying: on 5th December 1993 a lone whale was seen swimming and breaching 200 m off the coast of Corunha, Spain.

Blue Whale *Balaenoptera musculus*

F: Rorqual bleu
ESP: Ballena azul

Adult length: 24–30m
Group size: 1–2, sometimes more
Breaching: Only young known to breach, usually at 45° angle
Deep Dive: Sometimes raises tail flukes
Blow: Largest of all; an enormous vertical column up to 10m tall

IDENTIFICATION: The Blue Whale is the largest animal ever to have lived on Earth. The body is streamlined, with a broad head, rounded rostrum and large splashguard. The dorsal fin is very small relative to body size and is situated far along the back. The body colour is dark bluish-grey, mottled with light grey blotches. The blow is tall and vertical, often reaching a height of 10m.

SIMILAR SPECIES: At long range, or if poorly seen, this species can be confused with Fin Whale. Both are very large, with a tall, vertical blow and uniform greyish back. At relatively close range, Fin Whales appear darker, often with pale chevrons over the back, but without any pale mottling. Fin Whales also have a much more prominent dorsal fin which appears more rapidly after the blow-hole on surfacing.

BEHAVIOUR: Blue Whales are usually found singly or in pairs, although larger aggregations are found where there is a rich source of food. They occasionally show their flukes during deep dives, but only young animals have been observed breaching. They feed almost exclusively on krill.

STATUS AND DISTRIBUTION: Blue Whale has a world-wide distribution, with summer feeding grounds in cold sub-polar waters where krill is particularly abundant. However, whaling has severely depleted the population throughout its range. After a summer feasting, the whales migrate to tropical and sub-tropical waters in the winter, when breeding occurs. In the North Atlantic, small numbers are regularly recorded in the Gulf of St. Lawrence, Canada and around the coasts of western Iceland and Greenland. It is an extremely rare species in European waters. Recent records from the Bay of Biscay are few, but in August 1999 a single sub-adult was photographed off the north coast of Spain. This was followed by a spate of sightings during 1999 and summer 2000. New evidence suggests that there is a wintering population of over 50 animals in waters south-west of Ireland.

J F M A M J J A S O N D

PLATE 2

Sei Whale   *Balaenoptera borealis*

F: Rorqual boréal
ESP: Rorcual boreal

Adult length: 12–16 m
Group size: 1–2, sometimes more
Breaching: Seldom, generally rising at a low angle
Deep Dive: Does not raise tail flukes
Blow: Tall, thin and vertical, less robust than Fin Whale

IDENTIFICATION: Sei Whale is similar in form and colour to Fin Whale, but is smaller. It has an erect, sickle-shaped dorsal fin which appears proportionally larger than that of Fin Whale. A median ridge on the head extends from the blow-hole almost to the tip of the rostrum. When surfacing, the blow-hole and fin appear almost simultaneously. Also, whilst feeding, the back and dorsal fin are usually visible for a longer period compared with other rorquals. The blow is quite tall, but not as prominent as in Blue or Fin Whale.

SIMILAR SPECIES: This species can easily be confused with both Fin and Minke Whales. In general, a combination of features should be used to separate these species. Compared with Sei Whale, Fin Whale usually has a higher blow which appears well before the lower, sloping dorsal fin. Unlike Fin Whales, Sei Whales do not usually arch their tail-stock prior to a deep dive. At close range, the asymmetrical head pattern of Fin Whale is diagnostic. Minke Whales are distinguished from Sei Whales by their smaller size and lack of a prominent blow.

BEHAVIOUR: Sei Whales tend to travel alone or in pairs. Unlike other rorquals, they often skim-feed just below the surface. When feeding in this manner they can be quite unobtrusive, with only the occasional blow and top of the dorsal fin being visible. They are very fast swimmers, but do not appear to be as demonstrative as either Fin or Minke Whales.

STATUS AND DISTRIBUTION: Sei Whale has a cosmopolitan distribution, but appears to favour temperate to sub-polar waters. They are generally restricted to deep, pelagic waters and are rarely found near coasts. In Europe, small numbers are seen to the west of Britain and Ireland, and north to Iceland and northern Norway. This species appears to be a regular visitor to the Bay of Biscay, with variable numbers recorded each year over the shelf-edge and in deep water.

J F M A M J J A S O N D

Fin Whale   *Balaenoptera physalus*

F: Rorqual commun
ESP: Rorcual común

Adult length: 18–26 m
Group size: 1–5, sometimes more
Breaching: Variable angles, huge splash
Deep Dive: Tail flukes not raised
Blow: Tall column; thicker and higher than Sei, but smaller than Blue Whale

IDENTIFICATION: A large species, second only in size to Blue Whale. Fin Whale is a relatively slender, streamlined species with a pointed head and a prominent dorsal fin positioned three-quarters of the way along the back. The upperside of the body is dark grey, often with pale chevrons behind the blow-holes. At close range, the asymmetrical pigmentation of the lower jaw is diagnostic: the left lower lip being dark, the right being white. The tall, columnar blow often reaches a height of 8 m and takes several seconds to dissipate.

SIMILAR SPECIES: At long range confusion is likely with both Sei and Blue Whales. Sei Whales generally have a lower, more bushy blow, which, on surfacing, appears simultaneously with a more prominent sickle-shaped dorsal fin. Also, when diving, Fin Whales are more likely to arch their tail-stock. Blue Whales differ in having a small dorsal fin, paler coloration and mottled pattern. Unlike Blue Whales, Fin Whales only very rarely raise their tail flukes on diving.

BEHAVIOUR: Fin Whales are usually observed singly or in pairs, sometimes in small pods, and occasionally in large aggregations of up to 100 animals where food is plentiful. They are very fast swimmers and have been regularly recorded breaching and lunge-feeding.

STATUS AND DISTRIBUTION: Fin Whales are widely distributed throughout the world, but appear to be more common in sub-polar and cool temperate waters in the summer months, moving to warmer latitudes in the winter to mate and calve. The Fin Whale is the most abundant baleen whale in the region and is regularly recorded during the summer and early autumn in deep waters over the edge of the continental shelf. The Bay of Biscay appears principally to be a summer feeding ground for this species. However, of considerable interest was the birth of a calf in July 1999 in waters off northern Spain. Small numbers of well dispersed animals also occur throughout the winter.

J F M A M J J A S O N D

PLATE 3

Humpback Whale *Megaptera novaeangliae*

F: Mégaptère
ESP: Jorobada

Adult length: 11–15 m
Group size: 1–3, sometimes more
Breaching: Yes, usually landing on back
Deep Dive: Body generally arches high before broad tail flukes are raised to reveal variable pale underside to tail
Blow: Variable; tall, vertical and bushy

IDENTIFICATION: The Humpback is a large, stocky whale, black or dark grey in colour with a broad head covered in fleshy tubercles. One of the most distinctive features is the extremely long, mostly white, pectoral flippers. The dorsal fin is usually short and stubby. The blow is dense and mushroom-shaped. Before a sounding dive, the body usually arches steeply before the tail flukes are raised high above the surface. The trailing edge of the flukes is always irregular and the patterning on the underside can be used to identify individuals.

SIMILAR SPECIES: Although similar to several other rorquals in size, the distinctive flippers, fluke pattern and surfacing sequence separates the Humpback Whale from all other species.

BEHAVIOUR: Humpbacks can be very demonstrative and are regularly observed breaching, lob-tailing, and slapping their long flippers on the surface of the water. They are very vocal animals and are known as the singing whales. Although they usually travel singly or in very small pods, large congregations of animals commonly occur on the summer feeding grounds.

STATUS AND DISTRIBUTION: Humpback Whales are found throughout the world. During the summer months they feed in polar and cool temperate waters, migrating in the winter to sub-tropical and tropical latitudes, where they mate and calve. This species was heavily exploited by the whaling industry, but it now appears to be making a good recovery in many parts of the world. However, it is more common in the western North Atlantic and, away from Iceland, is still a relatively rare species in European waters. It is one of the rarest rorquals in the European Atlantic and has only been sighted on a few occasions in recent years.

Minke Whale *Balaenoptera acutorostrata*

F: Petit rorqual
ESP: Rorcual aliblanco

Adult length: 7–10 m
Group size: 1–2, occasionally more
Breaching: Variable angles
Deep Dive: Tail flukes not raised
Blow: Small, vertical and bushy, but usually not visible

IDENTIFICATION: The Minke Whale is the smallest baleen whale to be found in the European Atlantic. It has a slender, streamlined body with a pointed rostrum which is bisected by a single longitudinal ridge beginning in front of the blow-holes. The upperparts are dark grey, lightening to white on the belly and the underside of the flippers. A distinctive feature, although not often conspicuous in the field, is a diagonal white band on the upper surface of the flipper. The dorsal fin is tall and falcate and placed about two-thirds along the back. Minke Whales have an inconspicuous vertical blow, which is produced almost simultaneously with the appearance of the dorsal fin. When diving, they do not normally raise their tail flukes clear of the surface.

SIMILAR SPECIES: Confusion is most likely with the larger rorquals, particularly Sei and Fin Whales. However, the much smaller size and lack of a tall blow should distinguish it from these species. If seen poorly, Minke Whale may be confused with beaked whales, which are similar in size and shape although the pointed rostrum with a central ridge of Minke is diagnostic. Beaked whales tend to occur in much deeper waters than Minke Whales, although location alone should not be used to identify this species.

BEHAVIOUR: Minke Whales are usually solitary animals, sometimes seen in pairs or small groups, but rarely in larger aggregations. They can be very elusive and hard to follow when feeding actively. They are often quite inquisitive, occasionally approaching passing ships and turning on their sides as they swim past or lifting their heads clear of the surface. Breaching is regularly recorded, particularly during periods of rough weather.

STATUS AND DISTRIBUTION: Minke Whales have a world-wide distribution, but they appear to be more common in cooler waters than in the tropics. They are frequently seen during the summer and autumn in coastal waters around the British Isles, the Faroes, Iceland and western Norway. In the European Atlantic, the Minke Whale is most regularly recorded in the shelf waters off the Brittany coast. Most sightings have been of single animals during the summer months.

PLATE 4

Pygmy Sperm Whale *Kogia breviceps*

F: Cachalot pygmée
ESP: Cachalote pigmeo

Adult length: 2·7–3·7 m
Group size: 1–6
Breaching: Leaps vertically
Deep Dive: Tail flukes not raised
Blow: Blow-hole displaced slightly to the left. Blow low and faint

IDENTIFICATION: The diminutive size of the Pygmy Sperm Whale means that it is most likely to be mistaken for a dolphin or porpoise. However, in structure and behaviour it is quite unlike any of these species. Pygmy Sperm Whales are greyish in colour with a blunt, squarish head and a small, falcate dorsal fin.

SIMILAR SPECIES: The distinctive body shape and lethargic behaviour help to distinguish Pygmy Sperm Whale from similarly-sized dolphin species with relative ease. However, its similarity to Dwarf Sperm Whale means that many good sightings at sea fail to distinguish between the two species. Pygmy Sperm Whale differs from the slightly smaller Dwarf Sperm Whale by its smaller dorsal fin positioned further than half way along the back.

BEHAVIOUR: Pygmy Sperm Whales are typically seen moving slowly or hanging motionless at the surface. On diving, the body tends to sink below the surface, rather than rolling forward. When disturbed, sometimes emits a reddish-brown anal liquid to try and disorientate the intruder. Vertical breaches have been recorded.

STATUS AND DISTRIBUTION: Most information on the distribution of this species comes from strandings, which indicate that it occurs world-wide in deep temperate to tropical waters. Both Pygmy Sperm Whale and Dwarf Sperm Whale are often referred to as rare throughout their range, although the paucity of sightings may be due in part to their shy behaviour, small size and generally pelagic distribution. Prior to 1976, six strandings had been recorded along the Atlantic coast of France. From 1982 to 1990, there were five strandings along the north coast of Spain (the first for that coast), followed by two more on the Spanish Galician coast in 1995: on 20th October a 2·85 m female stranded on San Xurxo beach; and three days later another two females stranded on the same beach – one, 2·58 m in length was dead but the other, 1·40 m long, was successfully returned to the sea. Based on these few, widely distributed strandings, it seems possible that this species may occur regularly in the Bay of Biscay.

Pygmy Sperm Whales have yet to be observed at sea in the European Atlantic, but they have been recorded in adjacent waters on at least one occasion. In 1992 and 1993 the French albacore tuna fisheries working to the west of the Bay of Biscay carried researchers to record the number of accidental catches of cetaceans in fishing nets. They recorded a single entangled Pygmy Sperm Whale during their observations.

J F M A M J J A S O N D

Dwarf Sperm Whale *Kogia simus*

F: Cachalot nain
ESP: Cachalote enaño

Adult length: 2·1–2·8 m
Group size: 1–10
Breaching: Leaps vertically
Deep Dive: Tail flukes not raised
Blow: Blow-hole displaced slightly to the left. Blow low and faint

IDENTIFICATION: This poorly known species is almost identical to Pygmy Sperm Whale in form and colour. It is dolphin-sized, has a robust body, a short, rounded head and a small, underslung lower jaw. The blow-hole is positioned slightly to the left of the top of the head.

SIMILAR SPECIES: This small cetacean is superficially similar in size and shape to several species of dolphin but the blunt forehead lacking a beak, and generally lethargic behaviour are distinctive. Separation from Pygmy Sperm Whale is much more challenging, but Dwarf Sperm Whale is slightly smaller in size with a larger dorsal fin, which is broader at the base, and positioned centrally on the back.

BEHAVIOUR: Dwarf Sperm Whales occasionally breach, but they are more likely to be seen travelling slowly or resting at the surface. When disturbed they sometimes emit a reddish-black jet of ink as a defence mechanism.

STATUS AND DISTRIBUTION: Records of Dwarf Sperm Whale suggest a global distribution in deep-water temperate to tropical seas. Since there were only three records in European waters prior to 1993, it seems likely that this species is rare in the European Atlantic. Dwarf Sperm Whale is known from only two strandings in the European Atlantic. The first was a male in very shallow water near Port Louis on the southern coast of Brittany, France, on 24th October 1991. An attempt was made to return it to open water but it expelled a blackish liquid in defence and died. On 15th November 1999, another French stranding occured. This involved a young, 1·75 m long female which was discovered in the Gironde estuary (45° 40'N). Necropsy suggested that it probably died of septicemia.

J F M A M J J A S O N D

PLATE 5

Sperm Whale *Physeter macrocephalus*

F: Cachalot macrocephal
ESP: Cachalote

Adult length: 11–18 m
Group size: 1–20, sometimes more
Breaching: Leaps vertically
Deep Dive: Often arches body; usually raises dark, broad, triangular tail flukes vertically
Blow: Angled forward and to the left

IDENTIFICATION: The largest of the toothed whales: mature males average about 15 m in length; females about 10 m. The body is robust, with a massive, blunt head that comprises almost one-third of the animal's total length. The lower jaw is long, narrow and inconspicuous beneath the head. A single nostril is located on the left side of the front of the head, resulting in a distinctive 'forward' and angled blow. There is no dorsal fin, only a small hump, behind which are a series of knuckles running as far as the tail. Sperm Whales are normally slate grey or brown and the skin is usually wrinkled. The flukes, which are generally raised vertically prior to a sounding-dive, are large and triangular, with smooth edges and a deep central notch.

SIMILAR SPECIES: Sperm Whale overlaps with several rorquals in size and, like Humpback and Blue Whales, raises its flukes before sounding. However, all rorquals are distinguished by their vertical blow, rounded heads and distinctive dorsal fin.

BEHAVIOUR: Sperm Whales are gregarious, often travelling in pods of up to 20 or more, and are usually found in two distinct group types: mixed pods of females/immature males; and groups of bachelor males. They can be quite demonstrative and breach regularly, particularly on the breeding grounds. This species is renowned for diving to tremendous depths where it captures Giant Squid.

STATUS AND DISTRIBUTION: The Sperm Whale is widely distributed in deep, offshore waters throughout the world. The mixed pods of females and immature males usually remain in tropical or sub-tropical waters throughout the year. The groups of males travel to higher latitudes, sometimes as far as the icefields to feed, returning to join the groups of females during the breeding season. Records from the last few years indicate that small numbers of Sperm Whales visit the Bay of Biscay annually in late summer. These whales are usually solitary or occur in very small groups, which would suggest that they are predominantly males and probably migrating.

J F M A M J J A S O N D

Beaked whale identification

Six species of beaked whale (Ziphiidae) have occured in the European Atlantic. All of them are challenging to identify at sea, although the Northern Bottle-nosed Whale and Cuvier's Beaked Whale are distinctive given good views. By far the most difficult to identify of all the cetaceans in the European Atlantic are the *Mesoplodon* beaked whales, of which four are known to occur. As in other parts of the world, the vast majority of records are of strandings, where a positive identification is usually possible.

The sighting of a *Mesoplodon* beaked whale at sea is generally considered to be an exceptional event due to the shy habits, unobtrusive behaviour and apparent 'rarity' of all species throughout their known range in deep, offshore waters. It is, therefore, especially exciting that these whales are being sighted on several occasions annually in the southern Bay of Biscay. Unfortunately, because *Mesoplodon* beaked whales are so difficult to identify, most sightings are not recorded to species. There are still only a handful of photographs taken at sea, and photographs of stranded animals reveal little about their true coloration and nothing of their surfacing behaviour. The plate opposite illustrates the diagnostic features which are required to confirm identification of each species, based on current knowledge. It is important to note that, although the plate shows the whales raising their heads clear of the water, it is not known whether all of the species regularly do this when surfacing (although some have been seen to do so).

A close view of the head of an adult male is crucial to the positive identification of Gervais', True's and Sowerby's Beaked Whales. This is because only the mature males show a pair of protruding teeth, the only feature which reliably separates the three species. Fortunately, these are situated at different positions on each species, erupting at the tip of the jaw on True's, one-third of the way from the tip in Gervais', and half-way along the jaw in Sowerby's. Blainville's Beaked Whales are perhaps slightly easier to identify: whilst the body shape and coloration can be almost identical to the other species, adults generally show an arched lower jaw, from which a pair of protruding teeth erupt in males; in adult females, the tip of the jaw is often white.

Heads of *Mesoplodon* Beaked whales

f   **Blainville's Beaked Whale (female)** PLATE 7
raised jaw-line; jaw tip often white

m   **Blainville's Beaked Whale (male)** PLATE 7
arched lower jaw with erupting teeth

2   **True's Beaked Whale** PLATE 8
forehead tapering to a short, stubby beak; two protruding teeth at the tip of the lower jaw

3   **Gervais' Beaked Whale** PLATE 8
forehead tapering down to a shortish, slender beak; teeth emerge one-third of the way along the lower jaw

4   **Sowerby's Beaked Whale** PLATE 7
forehead tapering to a slender beak; teeth protrude mid-way along the lower jaw; the longest of the region's Mesoplodon species.

PLATE 6

Northern Bottle-nosed Whale *Hyperoodon ampullatus*

F: Hypéroodon boréal
ESP: Zifio boreal

Adult length: 7–9 m
Group size: 1–10
Breaching: Lifts entire body out of the water, sometimes several times in a single display
Deep Dive: Tail flukes not raised
Blow: Bushy, slightly angled forward; sometimes visible

IDENTIFICATION: Northern Bottle-nosed Whale is the largest species of beaked whale in the European Atlantic. It is medium-sized, uniform grey to brown in colour, and has a smallish, falcate dorsal fin situated two-thirds along the back. This species can only be reliably identified by viewing the large bulbous head as the animal breaks the surface. At close range, the rounded forehead can be seen to overhang slightly the short, protruding beak. The head often becomes paler on mature individuals.

SIMILAR SPECIES: Head-shape separates Northern Bottle-nosed Whale from the similar Cuvier's Beaked Whale and Minke Whale, although pod sizes of greater than two should generally eliminate Minke Whale.

BEHAVIOUR: Northern Bottle-nosed Whales are generally seen in pods moving slowly at the surface. Breaching has been observed occasionally.

STATUS AND DISTRIBUTION: This is the only species of beaked whale to be hunted commercially in the North Atlantic, with the depleted population finally being afforded protection in 1977. Northern Bottle-nosed Whales are restricted to the deep offshore waters of the northern North Atlantic, with the Bay of Biscay being towards the southernmost extent of their range. The Biscay population of this rare and little-studied cetacean seems to be centred over deep-water canyons of the Southern Bay, although it has been sighted farther north. Northern Bottle-nosed Whales were sighted regularly in the Bay of Biscay in 1998 and 1999, suggesting that this is the best place in the world to see this enigmatic species.

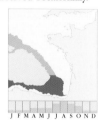

J F M A M J J A S O N D

Cuvier's Beaked Whale *Ziphius cavirostris*

F: Ziphius
ESP: Zifio común

Adult length: 5–7 m
Group size: 1–12
Breaching: Leaps almost vertically
Blow: Bushy, slightly angled forward; sometimes visible

IDENTIFICATION: Cuvier's Beaked Whale is one of the largest and most robust of the beaked whales. It is a medium-sized whale, with a longish back, small falcate dorsal fin and greyish to orange-brown coloration. It is best identified by its size, coloration and head-shape. The shape of the head and beak has been described as being like that of a goose, the forehead sloping gently to the tip of the short, but distinct, beak. Most observations do not provide views of the beak, but the gently curving forehead is quite unlike the bulbous melon which is characteristic of the other beaked whales. Mature adults sometimes develop completely pale heads, and, in some cases, this may extend along the back as far as the dorsal fin. The upper body is sometimes heavily scarred, possibly indicating that the individual concerned is an adult male which has been involved in fights. The blow is sometimes visible, up to 1 m tall and angled slightly forward.

SIMILAR SPECIES: Cuvier's Beaked Whale is similar in size and shape to Minke Whale and other beaked whales, but the head-shape distinguishes it from these species. Without the head-shape and pale coloration being seen, Cuvier's Beaked Whale cannot be reliably identified.

BEHAVIOUR: This scarce and poorly known whale has been sighted regularly in the region and recent observations have led to some new discoveries and exciting glimpses into its life history. Single mothers with young calves have been recorded on two occasions in the Bay of Biscay, suggesting that the area may be a calving ground. Apparently inquisitive animals have been recorded many times, often surfacing very close by, logging or moving slowly within a few tens of metres of the ship. Particularly pale, scarred animals are either seen alone, or at the head of pods of 5–10 darker animals. It is possible that these animals are sexually mature males which move between female pods as a mating strategy.

STATUS AND DISTRIBUTION: Stranding records suggest that Cuvier's Beaked Whale is cosmopolitan in temperate and tropical waters. In Europe, the species is regularly recorded from Ireland to the Mediterranean and has been seen throughout the deep waters of the Bay of Biscay, with the majority of records coming from the deep-water canyons of the Southern Bay.

J F M A M J J A S O N D

PLATE 7

Sowerby's Beaked Whale *Mesoplodon bidens*

F: Mésoplodon de Sowerby
ESP: Zifio de Sowerby

Adult length: 5–7 m
Group size: 1–8
Breaching: Leaps almost vertically
Blow: Bushy, slightly angled forward; sometimes visible

IDENTIFICATION: Although still only rarely sighted at sea, Sowerby's Beaked Whale is known from a number of photographs and close encounters. It is a small, slim whale, reminiscent in shape to an elongated dolphin. The dorsal fin is small, falcate and situated two-thirds of the way between the head and the tail. The upper surface is uniformly brown to grey, becoming paler towards the belly, and the eyes are often encircled by a dark patch. As with all beaked whales, identification at sea based on current knowledge is dependent upon observation of the head. The rounded forehead tapers to a slender beak, the length of which, although variable, is longer than the other beaked whales. The beak often breaks the water at a steep angle on surfacing and the observer must concentrate on this feature in an attempt to clinch identification. The only known diagnostic feature for this species at sea is the two flattened teeth that protrude mid-way along the lower jaw in adult males (*see Plate 5, page 26*).

SIMILAR SPECIES: Sowerby's Beaked Whale is almost identical in size and shape to Gervais', True's and Blainville's Beaked Whales and there is considerable overlap in coloration.

BEHAVIOUR: Sowerby's Beaked Whales are believed to be unobtrusive in their behaviour and generally shy of boats. However, breaching has been recorded on several occasions.

STATUS AND DISTRIBUTION: Sowerby's Beaked Whale is restricted to the northern North Atlantic, with the majority of sightings being at latitudes between the Canary Islands and the Arctic Circle. The Bay of Biscay is considered to be towards the southernmost limit of the species' range, with seven strandings along the French Atlantic coast between 1976 and 1999, and sightings of two adults on 22nd August 1995 and three adults on 23rd October 2000. Both sightings were in the Southern Bay. The status of Sowerby's Beaked Whale in the European Atlantic remains poorly known, but these few records suggest that it is the most frequently occurring *Mesoplodon* species in the region.

J F M A M J J A S O N D

Blainville's Beaked Whale *Mesoplodon densirostris*

F: Mésoplodon de Blainville
ESP: Zifio de Blainville

Adult length: 4–6 m
Group size: 1–6
Breaching: Unknown
Blow: Small blow projects forward, sometimes visible

IDENTIFICATION: Blainville's Beaked Whale is similar in size to the other *Mesoplodon* beaked whales. The body is reminiscent of an elongated dolphin, with a small, falcate to triangular dorsal fin, a flattish head, and uniform greyish-orange or brown coloration on the body. Mature Blainville's Beaked Whales can only be identified at sea by the unique shape of the beak (*see Plate 5, page 26*). The lower jaw is relatively short and distinctly arched, giving the impression, at a distance, of a bump on the forehead. In mature males, the arch is capped by two large, protruding teeth which are often encrusted in barnacles. This species often surfaces by first lifting its head out of the water. Therefore, whilst identification at sea is extremely difficult and would require exceptionally close views, the confirmation of a live sighting remains a real possibility.

SIMILAR SPECIES: Blainville's Beaked Whale overlaps in coloration and size with all of the other beaked whales. However, none of these species display the diagnostic raised jawline.

BEHAVIOUR: Blainville's Beaked Whales are believed to be unobtrusive in their behaviour.

STATUS AND DISTRIBUTION: Perhaps the most widespread *Mesoplodon* species, Blainville's Beaked Whale occurs throughout the world's oceans except the Arctic, with the great majority of records coming from the tropical Atlantic north to the Canary Islands. Within the European Atlantic, it is perhaps most likely to occur over the canyons of the Southern Bay, an area known to be favoured by this species and closest to its regular range. The stranding of a 4·35 m male at Tarnos, France on 8th January 1998 constituted the first record for France and the Bay of Biscay. This would suggest that these animals are very rare. Although the general paucity of strandings may disguise their actual distribution and abundance offshore.

J F M A M J J A S O N D

PLATE 8

True's Beaked Whale *Mesoplodon mirus*

F: Mésoplodon de True
ESP: Zifio de True

Adult length: 4–6 m
Group size: 1–6
Breaching: Unknown
Blow: Unknown

IDENTIFICATION: Like Gervais' Beaked Whale, True's Beaked Whale is known from only a handful of stranding records and encounters at sea. There is consequently much to learn about its identification, behaviour and ecology. One of the two encounters known to have been photographed was off North Carolina, USA and involved three small, slim whales. Their backs were grey with a dark ridge and much darker dorsal fins. One of the animals had a falcate dorsal fin, whilst the other two whale's fins were almost triangular. The head in front of the blow-hole was distinctly bulbous, with a dark patch around the eye and a short stubby beak. No teeth were seen and the pod was considered to consist of two females and a calf (*see Plate 5, page 26*).

SIMILAR SPECIES: True's Beaked Whales are extremely similar to other *Mesoplodon* beaked whales, making identification at sea almost impossible without good views of the head.

BEHAVIOUR: With only a handful of sightings ever made at sea, its behaviour remains relatively unknown. There is evidence that True's Beaked Whale breaches regularly but it is likely that it generally avoids boats and moves unobtrusively at the surface.

STATUS AND DISTRIBUTION: The vast majority of stranding records for this species are from the North Atlantic, although animals have also stranded in South Africa and Australia. In Europe, a few strandings have occurred on the coasts of Spain, France, Ireland and the Canary Islands.

There has been one stranding recorded in the Bay of Biscay: a single animal on the north coast of Spain in 1981. Subsequently, an individual which was believed to be this species was recorded in the Bay of Biscay. This mature individual breached five times close to the ship; the greyish hue of its body, gently sloping forehead and short beak were noted. On 9th September 1999, a carbon-copy of the first sighting occurred. On this occasion, the animal breached 17 times to the amazement of the onlooking observers.

J F M A M J J A S O N D

Gervais' Beaked Whale *Mesoplodon europaeus*

F: Mésoplodon de Gervais
ESP: Zifio de Gervais

Adult length: 4·6–6 m
Group size: Unknown
Breaching: Unknown
Blow: Unknown

IDENTIFICATION: The pelagic distribution, shy habits and the difficulty in identifying Gervais' Beaked Whale means that it has hardly ever been recorded with certainty at sea. Based on a number of strandings and one photograph of a live animal from the Canary Islands, it is known to be a slim, medium-sized whale, like an elongated dolphin, with a small falcate to triangular dorsal fin. The upper surface is dark grey, fading to paler below, and the eye is often encircled by a dark patch. On surfacing, the beak is raised distinctly out of the water. Like the other *Mesoplodon* beaked whales, good views of the head are essential to confirm identification. The small forehead curves gently down to a shortish, slender beak. In adult males, a pair of teeth emerge one-third of the way along the lower jaw. This is the only known diagnostic identification feature for the species (*see Plate 5, page 26*).

SIMILAR SPECIES: Similar in size, shape and coloration to other beaked whales. Beak length is generally considered to be intermediate between the stubby beak of True's Beaked Whale and the long, slender beak of Sowerby's Beaked Whale. However, the lack of sightings may be the reason for other identification features not yet being known.

BEHAVIOUR: The only observations of Gervais' Beaked Whale in recent times have come from the Azores and Canary Islands. Due to uncertainty about the identity of most sightings, details of behaviour have yet to be confirmed. The lack of sightings does, however, suggest that this species is probably unobtrusive and shy.

STATUS AND DISTRIBUTION: Gervais' Beaked Whale is almost completely unknown at sea. It has been photographed and identified alive on only one occasion – close to the Canary Islands. Most of our limited knowledge of this species therefore comes from a handful of strandings. The species' stronghold appears to be in the western North Atlantic and there are few European records. However, its occurrence in the Bay of Biscay was confirmed when a 4·09m long male stranded at Biscarrosse, France (44°20'N) on 16th January 1999. Previous to this, the only record for the European Atlantic was a dead individual found floating in the English Channel in 1840.

J F M A M J J A S O N D

True's Beaked Whale, digital illustration based on the description of the North Carolina individuals

e: True's Beaked Whale, two photographs of an individual believed to be this species from the Azores

PLATE 9

Rough-toothed Dolphin *Steno bredanensis*

F: Stèno
ESP: Steno

Adult length: 2·1–2·6 m
Group size: 1–50
Behaviour: Sometimes shows a characteristic swimming pattern described as 'skimming across the surface'

IDENTIFICATION: A fairly robust dolphin. The head-shape is distinctive, being conical with a low melon and long, slender beak. There is no distinct differentiation between the beak and the forehead as in other long-beaked dolphins, giving this species a slightly reptilian appearance. The dorsal fin is wide at the base, and pointed but not hooked. The upper-back is dark grey, forming a cape, becoming lighter towards the flanks which often have white or pinkish blotches. The belly and undersides of the tail-stock are usually white. The beak may also show whitish or pinkish patches, particularly around the lips.

SIMILAR SPECIES: The wholly dark grey body and fairly large size makes this species very similar to Bottle-nosed Dolphin. However, when seen well, the distinctive head structure and dark cape should distinguish Rough-toothed Dolphin from the latter species.

BEHAVIOUR: This is a relatively poorly known dolphin which has been seen most frequently in groups of between 10 and 20, although pods of over 100 have been reported. It does not appear to be a particularly active species, but will often ride the bow-wave of ships. Occasionally when swimming at high speed, Rough-toothed Dolphins hold their heads and chins above the surface of the water, in a characteristic behaviour described as 'skimming'.

STATUS AND DISTRIBUTION: Rough-toothed Dolphins have a world-wide distribution in tropical, sub-tropical and warm temperate waters. They are normally found in deep waters beyond the edge of the continental shelf. In Europe, this species is regularly seen around the Canary Islands and occasionally in the Azores. There are no documented sightings at sea in the region, but two strandings have occurred on the Atlantic coast of France. It is likely that this species only occurs very rarely in the Bay of Biscay, perhaps during warm water years.

Bottle-nosed Dolphin *Tursiops truncatus*

F: Grand dauphin
ESP: Delfín de dientes rugosos

Adult length: 1·9–3·9 m
Group size: 1–50
Behaviour: Highly active, capable of great speed and amazing acrobatics

IDENTIFICATION: A large, robust dolphin which, due to its widespread use in aquaria and popularity with the media, is one of the most familiar of all the cetaceans. Body coloration is uniformly grey above, fading to paler grey flanks and a lighter, sometimes pinkish, belly. The dorsal fin is centrally-placed, tall and falcate.

SIMILAR SPECIES: The large size, plain grey coloration, and lack of distinct flank markings distinguishes this species from most other dolphins. Confusion is possible with the Rough-toothed Dolphin and the Harbour Porpoise (Plate 14). However, the distinct bulging forehead and short, stubby beak should help to separate it from the former, and the falcate dorsal fin from the latter.

BEHAVIOUR: This species is most commonly seen in groups of between five and 50 individuals, which on occasion join other dolphin groups to form larger pods numbering several hundred animals. These large congregations regularly include other species of dolphin, including Short-finned and Long-finned Pilot Whales. They are very active and curious animals and are capable of travelling at great speed. Bottle-nosed Dolphins regularly ride in the bow-wave and wake of passing ships and are capable of amazing acrobatics.

STATUS AND DISTRIBUTION: This cosmopolitan species occurs throughout temperate and tropical seas. In most areas, including the European Atlantic, there seems to be two population types, nearshore and offshore, which probably never interbreed. The nearshore type can be found in bays, lagoons and estuaries, while the offshore type ranges more widely in shelf waters and pelagic waters beyond the continental slope. The offshore type is regularly seen in shelf waters to the south of the Brittany peninsula. Small numbers of the inshore type are recorded along the south coast of England, the west coast of France, and the north coast of Spain, where they have even been seen regularly in Santander harbour.

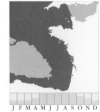

J F M A M J J A S O N D

PLATE 10

Common Dolphin *Delphinus delphis*

F: Dauphin commun
ESP: Delfín común

Adult length: 1·7–2·5 m
Group size: Generally 1–500
Behaviour: Highly active, fast swimmer capable of impressive acrobatics

IDENTIFICATION: A streamlined dolphin with a long, slender, dark beak and a tall, falcate dorsal fin. The main identification feature is a characteristic, 'figure-of-eight' pattern on the flanks. At close range, the anterior half of the 'figure-of-eight' appears tawny-yellow or brown and the posterior half grey. The dark colour of the back extends down into the central part of the 'figure-of-eight' to form a distinctive 'point' directly below the dorsal fin. Close views also reveal a thin black stripe extending from the flipper to the beak and a further dark stripe running from the eye to the beak. The central part of the dorsal fin is often pale.

SIMILAR SPECIES: This species, if seen distantly or in poor weather conditions, may be mistaken for Striped Dolphin due to its similar size and shape. However, the distinctive flank pattern is the best way of distinguishing Common Dolphin from all other species.

BEHAVIOUR: Common Dolphins are fast, energetic swimmers and are readily attracted to the bow-wave and wake of passing ships. They are frequently observed porpoising clear of the water. This species is sometimes seen in huge pods numbering thousands of animals, but in the European Atlantic the average pod size is 20, with the largest pods containing about 500. Common Dolphins sometimes associate with other species, principally with Striped Dolphins, but occasionally with Bottle-nosed Dolphins and pilot whales.

STATUS AND DISTRIBUTION: Common Dolphin has a world-wide distribution in tropical, sub-tropical and temperate zones, and is found both in shelf waters and beyond the edge of the continental shelf. It is the most abundant cetacean in the region and appears to be widespread. Unsurprisingly, it is also the species most commonly stranded on the Atlantic coasts of France, Spain and south-west England. There have been several mass strandings in recent years along French and English coastlines. The deaths of these dolphins have been linked to accidental capture in trawler nets.

J F M A M J J A S O N D

Striped Dolphin *Stenella coeruleoalba*

F: Dauphin bleu et blanc
ESP: Delfín listado

Adult length: 1·8–2·5 m
Group size: Generally 10–500
Behaviour: Perhaps even more acrobatic than Common Dolphin, often cautious around boats, swimming in tightly packed pod

IDENTIFICATION: A slender species, with a gently sloping forehead, dark, prominent beak and a slightly hooked, triangular dorsal fin. Similar in size and shape to Common Dolphin. The upperparts are dark blue-grey, with a distinctive pale blaze that sweeps from the flank back and up towards the dorsal fin. A thin, dark stripe runs along the lower flanks from the eye to the underside of the tail-stock. This stripe can be difficult to see unless the dolphin jumps clear of the surface. The underparts from the throat to the base of the tail-stock are white or pinkish.

SIMILAR SPECIES: In poor light, or at long range, Striped Dolphin can be quite difficult to distinguish from Common Dolphin. Both species are broadly similar in size and shape and cannot be separated unless the distinctive flank patterning is seen.

BEHAVIOUR: A very demonstrative species, Striped Dolphins are often seen leaping clear of the water or moving quickly towards the bow or wake of passing vessels. In the European Atlantic, pods average 25 individuals, but can number as many as 200. This species is regularly seen in association with feeding Fin Whales, sometimes riding the bow-wave created by the enormous whales as they surface. Striped Dolphins are often cautious, moving slowly in a tightly-packed pod, when in the vicinity of vessels, before speeding up and leaping high in a fit of energy once the ship has passed.

STATUS AND DISTRIBUTION: The Striped Dolphin has a world-wide distribution, but is confined to tropical, sub-tropical and warm temperate waters. It is generally pelagic, preferring deep water beyond the edge of the continental shelf. This is one of the most abundant dolphin species in the European Atlantic and is regularly recorded in offshore waters south of 47°N. However, a very small number of animals are also seen in coastal waters off north-west France and south-west England, and the species regularly strands along the Atlantic coasts of France and Spain. These strandings generally occur during the winter months and have been linked to accidental capture in fishing nets.

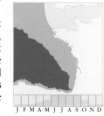

J F M A M J J A S O N D

PLATE 11

Atlantic White-sided Dolphin *Lagenorhynchus acutus*

F: Dauphin á flancs blanc
ESP: Delfín de flancos blancos

Adult length: 2·0–2·8 m
Group size: 1–500
Behaviour: Acrobatic and energetic, breaches, lob-tails, follows boats

IDENTIFICATION: A large, robust dolphin with a markedly thick tail-stock. It has a tall, sickle-shaped dorsal fin situated halfway along the back. The principal identification feature is the sharply-defined white patch on the flanks which extends along the tail-stock as an elongated yellow stripe. The short beak, back and dorsal fin are dark-coloured; the flanks are pale grey; and the belly white.

SIMILAR SPECIES: At long range, this species could be confused with several other dolphins. Although, when seen, the yellow or tan flank stripe is diagnostic. The most likely confusion species is the similarly-sized White-beaked Dolphin, which also has a prominent, falcate dorsal fin. However, unlike the Atlantic White-sided Dolphin, this species has white or pale dorsal markings in front of and behind the dorsal fin.

BEHAVIOUR: A very acrobatic and energetic species which often exhibits exuberant breaching and lob-tailing displays. They are regularly encountered in pods numbering up to 50 animals, but larger groups of several hundred individuals are not uncommon.

STATUS AND DISTRIBUTION: The Atlantic White-sided Dolphin is confined to the cool temperate and sub-arctic waters of the North Atlantic. In Europe, it is regularly recorded during the summer months in offshore waters to the west of Britain and Ireland, north to the Faroes, Iceland and western Norway. This is one of the scarcest species of dolphin to occur in the European Atlantic, with the waters off northern Spain representing the southernmost extent of its range. They have only been recorded twice since 1995, and only a very small number of animals strand on the Atlantic coasts of France and Spain each year.

J F M A M J J A S O N D

White-beaked Dolphin *Lagenorhynchus albirostris*

F: Dauphin á bec blanc
ESP: Delfín de hocico blanco

Adult length: 2–3 m
Group size: 1–20
Behaviour: Fast swimmer, regularly breaching and lob-tailing; follows boats

IDENTIFICATION: A large and very robust dolphin with a short, thick rounded beak and thick tail-stock. One of the most useful identification features is the white or pale grey markings on the flanks. The most distinctive of these markings is a pale grey area which extends from the upper flanks in front of the dorsal fin towards the tail-stock, and onto the back behind the dorsal fin, giving the impression of a pale 'saddle'. The belly is white as far back as the tail-stock. The dorsal fin is tall and sickle-shaped. The beak is usually, although not always, pale-grey or white.

SIMILAR SPECIES: At a distance, this species could be mistaken for several other dolphins, but confusion is most likely with its close relative the Atlantic White-sided Dolphin. However, the latter species can be distinguished by the long, discrete, oval-shaped white patch on the flanks, which extends along the tail-stock as a yellow band. In addition, Atlantic White-sided Dolphins do not have a pale 'saddle' behind the dorsal fin.

BEHAVIOUR: The White-beaked Dolphin is a fast and powerful swimmer, which can be very active and has regularly been observed breaching and lob-tailing. Like many other dolphins, it is not shy and will ride in the bow-waves and wakes of ships, boats or even large whales. Rarely seen alone, White-beaked Dolphins tend to occur in small pods, with up to 20 individuals being recorded together in the European Atlantic.

STATUS AND DISTRIBUTION: This species is confined to the cool and sub-arctic waters of the North Atlantic. In Europe, it is most commonly found around the coasts of northern Britain, north to Iceland. The coastal waters off northern Spain represent the southernmost limit of this species' range. White-beaked Dolphins have only been recorded on a few occasions, over the shelf and shelf-edge of the Bay of Biscay.

J F M A M J J A S O N D

PLATE 12

Long-finned Pilot Whale   *Globicephala melaena*

F: Globicéphale noir
ESP: Calderon común

Adult length: 3·5–6·5 m
Group size: Family groups of 2–50
Breaching: Various angles
Blow: Distinctly bushy

IDENTIFICATION: The Long-finned Pilot Whale is easily identified from all but the Short-finned Pilot Whale by its distinctive shape and behaviour. On surfacing, the bulbous, rounded head and distinct bushy blow precedes a robust body with the dorsal fin set well forward on the back. Behind the dorsal fin, the back and tail-stock are long. In mature males and females, the dorsal fin is distinctly broad-based, but the fin is most striking in males in which it broadens to a flag shape. Mature males also develop broad, muscular shoulders as they age. Immature animals have pointed, dolphin-like dorsal fins, which, being positioned relatively close to the head, should distinguish them from most other dolphin species. Coloration is a glossy black, with a narrow white underbelly. Long-finned Pilot Whales feed mostly at night, spending much of the day travelling slowly or logging at the surface.

SIMILAR SPECIES: The only reliable way of distinguishing Long-finned from Short-finned Pilot Whale is on the length of the pectoral flippers. Flipper length varies in both species but averages 16% of body length in Short-finned compared with 22% in Long-finned.

BEHAVIOUR: These whales are usually seen in family groups, resting or moving leisurely. They are inquisitive animals and often appear close to ships, sometimes tail-slapping, flipper-slapping, spy-hopping, or breaching. Long-finned Pilot Whales regularly associate with Common and Bottle-nosed Dolphins.

STATUS AND DISTRIBUTION: This species is very common in all cold temperate to sub-polar waters, with the exception of the North Pacific. In European waters, they are regularly seen inshore and offshore between Iceland and North Africa. Because the ranges of Long-finned and Short-finned Pilot Whales overlap in the Bay of Biscay, and because specific identification is very difficult at sea, observations should generally be recorded simply as 'pilot whale'. However, since Short-finned Pilot Whales are considered to be extremely rare in the Bay of Biscay, it is likely that the vast majority of sightings are of Long-finned Pilot Whale. The majority of sightings in the European Atlantic occur in deep water, but seasonal inshore movements regularly take place. In 1997, large numbers were seen off the Brittany coast during a period when hundreds of dead cuttlefish were observed. The whales may have been following this prey species inshore.

J F M A M J J A S O N D

Short-finned Pilot Whale   *Globicephala macrorhynchus*

F: Globicéphale tropical
ESP: Calderon tropical

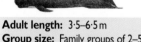

Adult length: 3·5–6·5 m
Group size: Family groups of 2–50
Breaching: Occasional, various angles
Blow: Distinctly bushy

IDENTIFICATION: Short-finned Pilot Whales, like Long-finned Pilot Whales, are fairly distinctive at sea. They give the impression of a large, robust, black dolphin with a bulbous head, broad dorsal fin situated well forward on the back, and a long tail-stock. A pale 'saddle' behind the dorsal fin, and various pale markings are often present on the back. They exhibit a low, bushy blow whilst travelling, and their behaviour is similar to that of Long-finned Pilot Whales, usually occurring in family pods and generally resting during the day and feeding at night.

SIMILAR SPECIES: Reliable identification from Long-finned Pilot Whale requires exceptional views of the short flippers which are generally less than one-fifth of the body length. Some researchers suggest that the pale 'saddle' occurs far more regularly in Short-finned, but this feature cannot be used alone in identification. Short-finned Pilot Whale has yet to be positively identified at sea in the European Atlantic.

BEHAVIOUR: The behaviour of Short-finned Pilot Whales at the surface is almost identical to that of Long-finned Pilot Whales. These whales are almost always seen in family groups travelling slowly at the surface or logging. On sighting a group, it is generally worth scanning other areas of sea as small groups are often spread out over a few kilometres. Other behaviours such as spy-hopping and flipper-slapping frequently occur. Short-finned Pilot Whales often associate with dolphins, particularly Common Dolphin and Bottle-nosed Dolphin.

STATUS AND DISTRIBUTION: Short-finned Pilot Whales are most commonly distributed in tropical and sub-tropical waters between 40°N and 40°S, well south of the Bay of Biscay. However, between 1982 and 1986, ten pilot whales stranded on the north coast of Spain were positively identified as Short-finned, bringing into question the northern geographical limit of the species, which may be around 45°N in the Bay of Biscay.

J F M A M J J A S O N D

PLATE 13

False Killer Whale *Pseudorca crassidens*

F: Faux-orque
ESP: Orca falsa

Adult length: 4–6 m
Group size: 2–200
Breaching: Frequent, various angles
Blow: Inconspicuous and bushy

IDENTIFICATION: False Killer Whales are large, elegant, and extremely active predators. They are typically seen in family groups, racing powerfully at the surface with their heads and upper bodies raised above the water. At other times, they travel at a more leisurely pace. Although False Killer Whales are often seen in association with other cetaceans, such as Bottle-nosed Dolphins, they have frequently been recorded attacking a range of different cetacean species, including the mighty Sperm Whale. Pod sizes are generally fairly small, although several hundred have been seen together on occasion.

SIMILAR SPECIES: Confusion is perhaps most likely with female or immature pilot whales or Orca. The slender, tapering head, slim body and dorsal fin placed centrally on the back, distinguish it from the former, whilst the all-dark body distinguishes it from the latter.

STATUS AND DISTRIBUTION: Although widely distributed throughout the tropical and warm temperate oceans of the world, the False Killer Whale seems to be fairly uncommon throughout its range. Whilst this species has been recorded as far north as the UK, the northern limit of its regular range in the Atlantic appears to be around the Straits of Gibraltar. False Killer Whales are scarce visitors to the Bay of Biscay, with only two sightings in deep waters along the shelf-edge in the southern Bay. On 16th October 1997, a pod of seven surfaced close to the ferry, swam along the stern, then turned swiftly and headed away. On 17th August 1998, another pod was sighted, involving just 3 animals, again swimming close to the ship.

J F M A M J J A S O N D

Orca or Killer Whale *Orcinus orca*

F: Orque
ESP: Orca

Adult length: 5–9 m
Group size: Family groups of 2–30
Breaching: Leaps vertically
Blow: Tall and bushy

IDENTIFICATION: The largest of the blackfish, the Orca is perhaps the most striking and familiar cetacean of all. The stocky, sleek, black body, white eye patch, and prominent dorsal fin are unmistakable. Fin shape and size varies depending on the age and sex of the individual. Adult males are the most distinctive, with broad, triangular dorsal fins reaching up to 2 m in height. Females and immatures are significantly shorter in body length, with smaller, sickle-shaped dorsal fins. Most animals show a clear grey 'saddle' patch behind the dorsal fin. Orcas spend most of their lives in discrete family groups of two or more animals, so most sightings involve individuals with different shaped dorsal fins. These powerful predators are capable of swimming at high speed and regularly spy-hop and breach.

SIMILAR SPECIES: In poor light, or at long range, when the white eye patch is not visible, it is possible to mistake female or immature Orcas for other members of the blackfish family or large dolphins such as Risso's Dolphin.

BEHAVIOUR: In some regions Orcas are known regularly to attack large baleen whales. This is the reason for whalers in the southern ocean giving them the name whale killers, hence their alternative present day name of Killer Whales. A memorable sighting occurred on 3rd August 1998, when a pod of five were seen in association with four Fin Whales. The Orca pod may have been hunting the Fin Whales, possibly targeting a calf which was observed within the group. For the duration of the sighting, the young Fin Whale was positioned between the larger, adult Fin Whales and the Orcas. In August 1999, another exciting interaction was observed in which two bull Orcas were seen in apparent pursuit of two adult pilot whales, before all four animals dived under the bow of the ship.

STATUS AND DISTRIBUTION: Records in the European Atlantic would suggest that Orcas are scarce visitors in deep water over the continental shelf-edge. However, previous research in shelf waters off the north coast of Spain suggests that the species may occur with some regularity. There have been records of live strandings of pilot whales and Common Dolphins, with Orcas in the vicinity, supporting the theory that Orcas in the Bay of Biscay may hunt other marine mammals as part of their regular diet.

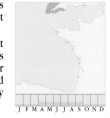

J F M A M J J A S O N D

PLATE 14

Risso's Dolphin   *Grampus griseus*

F: Dauphin de Risso
ESP: Delfín gris

Adult length: 2·6–3·8 m

Group size: 1–15

Behaviour: Can be energetic but more frequently engages in slow travel or logging. Displays many behaviours including spy-hopping lob-tailing and breaching

IDENTIFICATION: The distinctive shape and coloration of Risso's Dolphin means that it is unlikely to be mistaken at close range. Initial impressions are of a large, robust dolphin with a tall, falcate dorsal fin. Closer examination should reveal the distinctive bulbous head with a short, indistinct beak, uniform dark grey to pale grey coloration, and extensive scarring on the body. The scarring is the product of battles with other Risso's Dolphins. Adults become paler and more heavily scarred with age, although the dorsal fin and adjacent back often remain distinctly darker.

SIMILAR SPECIES: Views of the bulbous forehead, with a lack of a distinctive beak, cream coloration and extensive scarring allow the observer to discount all other dolphins in the region. Surprisingly, perhaps, the most likely confusion species in good light is Cuvier's Beaked Whale, mature individuals of which are the only other cetacean which can appear extensively cream coloured and scarred on the upper surface. However, the tall, centrally-placed dorsal fin and bulbous head-shape of Risso's Dolphin is clearly different. Risso's Dolphins are also similar in shape to several members of the blackfish family, particularly pilot whales, with which they often associate. Several of the above features should be noted to distinguish them in poor light.

BEHAVIOUR: Risso's Dolphins feed mainly on fish and squid at night, and spend much of the day engaged in slow travel or logging at the surface. They are highly inquisitive animals and often breach, spy-hop, and tail-slap. Most sightings in the European Atlantic involve animals milling leisurely at the surface, completely unconcerned by the close proximity of the ship.

STATUS AND DISTRIBUTION: Risso's Dolphins have a world-wide tropical to warm temperate distribution, the northern limit of their regular range being in the North Atlantic around the Shetland Islands. In the Bay of Biscay, sightings have been made in all regions and water depths, but encounters are infrequent. Pod sizes in the Bay of Biscay and elsewhere in Europe generally involve between one and 15 individuals.

J F M A M J J A S O N D

Harbour Porpoise   *Phocoena phocoena*

F: Marsoin commun
ESP: Marsopa

Adult length: 1·5–1·7 m

Group size: 1–6

Behaviour: Slow swimmers, unobtrusive, shy, rarely approach boats, usually moving away

IDENTIFICATION: The Harbour Porpoise is the smallest cetacean occurring in the European Atlantic. It has a robust body, small, rounded head and no beak. The most obvious identification feature is the centrally-placed dorsal fin which is small, low and triangular in shape. The upperparts of the body are dark grey, merging to lighter grey on the flanks; the underside of the body is white. Calves and juveniles often have brownish backs.

SIMILAR SPECIES: At long range, this species may be confused with Bottle-nosed Dolphin, which also shows a centrally-placed dorsal fin and uniform grey upperparts. However, when seen well, the diminutive size, distinctive shape of the dorsal fin, and unobtrusive behaviour should distinguish the Harbour Porpoise from all other cetaceans in the region.

BEHAVIOUR: Harbour Porpoises are sighted alone or in small groups and generally travel quite slowly. They are unobtrusive and very difficult to observe in rough weather. Unlike many dolphin species, Harbour Porpoises are shy and rarely approach boats; indeed they often move away from approaching ships.

STATUS AND DISTRIBUTION: The Harbour Porpoise is predominantly a coastal species, favouring shallow waters over the continental shelf. It is restricted to the cold temperate and sub-arctic waters of the Northern Hemisphere. In the eastern North Atlantic, it ranges from Iceland south to the coasts of Senegal, including the North and Baltic Seas and the western Mediterranean.

This species is recorded on a regular basis around the Brittany Coast and the western approaches to the English Channel. Congregations in early August regularly peak at 60-100 feeding animals, suggesting that this area is of international importance for the species. In general, the European population has declined significantly in the last 30 years due to increased levels of pollution, loss of prey through over-fishing and accidental capture in fishing nets.

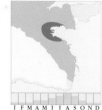

J F M A M J J A S O N D

Surfacing sequences of larger whales

The illustrations in this section show, from left to right, the sequence of appearance of the blow, head, upper back and, for some species, the tail flukes at the surface for the larger whales. The shape and patterning of the underside of the tail flukes for the four species that regularly raise their tail before diving are illustrated below.

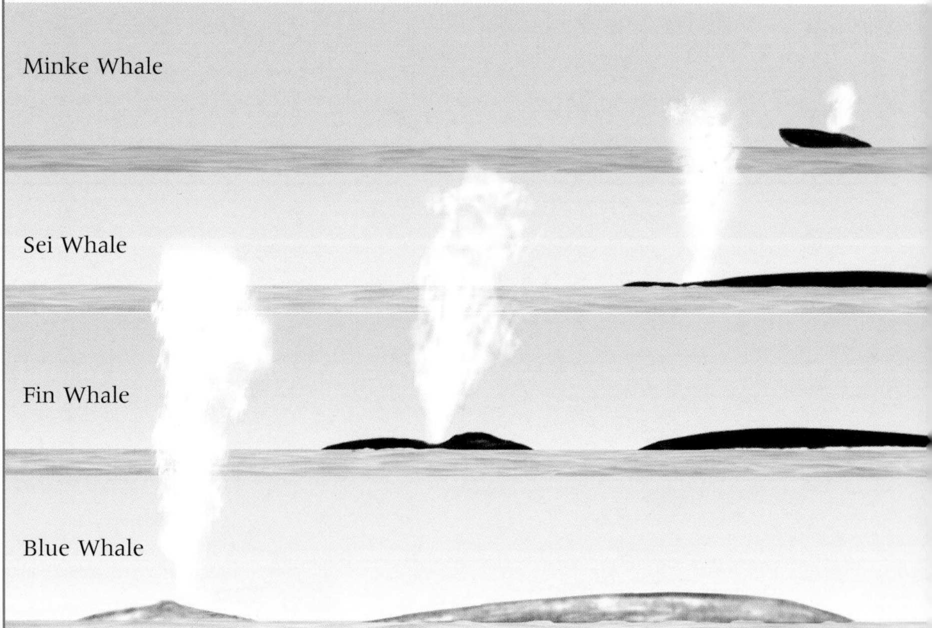

Blue Whale

Sperm Whale

Northern Right Whale

Humpback Whale

Sperm Whale

Northern Right Whale

Humpback Whale

Minke Whale

Sei Whale

Fin Whale

Blue Whale

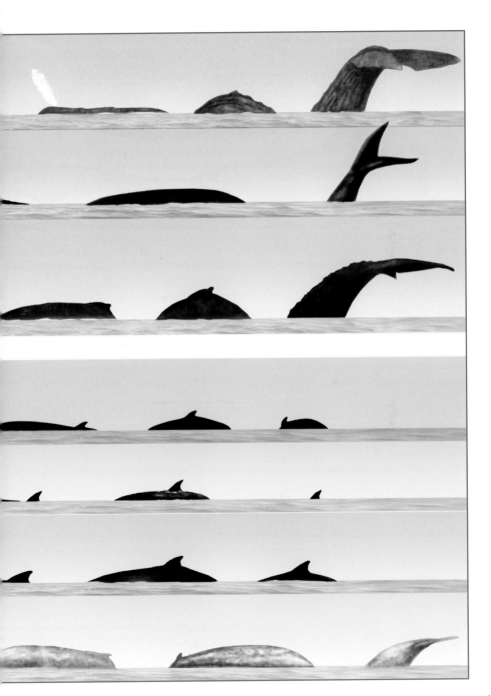

Other marine life

The European Atlantic supports a wealth of marine life ranging from the tiniest phytoplankton to the mighty Blue Whale. Whales and dolphins are amongst the most obvious signs of ocean life because of their size and need to return to the surface to breathe. However, there are many other interesting creatures for ocean-going wildlife enthusiasts to look out for. When searching for cetaceans it is easy to get into the habit of scanning the surface at a distance on the presumption that closer surfacing cetaceans will be picked up in the periphery of the eye's vision. Unfortunately this often results in smaller objects close to the boat being overlooked and it is therefore worthwhile looking down into the water from time to time.

The surface zone of the ocean plays host to a number of interesting shark species. Blue Shark, Mako Shark and Porbeagle are regularly seen in the European Atlantic. But by far the largest and most regularly identified species is the Basking Shark, which can reach a length of 13 m. Basking Sharks occur regularly in shelf waters from mid to late summer. Their large, triangular dorsal fin is usually the first sign of their presence, and the tail fin also breaks the surface, moving from side to side as the animal swims forward.

Another large and rather strange-looking creature that is regularly encountered in the European Atlantic is the Ocean Sunfish. Looking more like a giant dinner plate than a fish, they are often seen basking at the surface on sunny days.

Several species of tuna occur in the European Atlantic, ranging in size from less than 0·5 m to the size of dolphins, and, like dolphins, they often leap high out of the water. The larger species often associate with dolphin pods and may hunt alongside them. Unfortunately, this has led to the capture of large numbers of dolphins in tuna fishing nets in some areas.

Turtles are also regularly seen at the surface during the summer. The Leatherback is the most likely species to be encountered and is readily identified by the distinctive longitudinal ridges on its carapace. Other species less commonly recorded include Green and Loggerhead Turtles.

Seabirds, such as shearwaters, petrels, Northern Gannet, gulls and auks are perhaps the most visible inhabitants of the marine environment. They often provide useful clues as to the whereabouts of whales and dolphins as they tend to gather in areas where there is an abundance of food close to the surface. Some seabirds, such as Northern Gannet, may actually follow dolphins as they hunt, hoping for the opportunity to catch a fish forced to the surface.

Ocean Sunfish

Topographical map of the region

Showing depth, sea areas, regions referred to in this book and the approximate routes of the ferries.

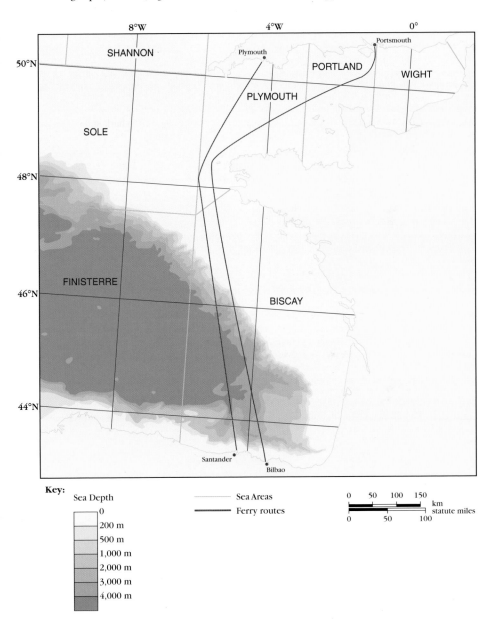

Key:

Sea Depth

	0
	200 m
	500 m
	1,000 m
	2,000 m
	3,000 m
	4,000 m

Sea Areas

Ferry routes

Conservation and research

During the summers of 1995 and 1996, a small group of observers carried out three reconnaissance surveys of the English Channel and Bay of Biscay. Two passenger ferries that sail between England and northern Spain were used as survey vessels: the Pride of Bilbao (P&O Portsmouth) which runs throughout the year between Portsmouth and Bilbao; and the Val de Loire (Brittany Ferries) which sails from Plymouth to Santander between March and November. A total of 14 species of cetacean was observed during these surveys, including several rarely seen beaked whales, along with large numbers of Fin Whales and Common Dolphins. The high density of cetaceans and the diversity of species encountered on these trips surprised most of the observers and encouraged them to set up a series of transect surveys the following year. In 1997 and 1998, volunteer observers carried out a further 24 cetacean transect surveys from the above ferries. The principal aim of the surveys was to obtain information on the status and distribution of cetaceans in the English Channel and eastern half of the Bay of Biscay. An additional objective was to inform the general public of the great potential the ferries offered for watching whales and dolphins so close to the United Kingdom. The surveys proved to be a great success and the sightings were collated and later published in the 1997 and 1998 Bay of Biscay Cetacean Reports.

Following publication of the 1998 Bay of Biscay Cetacean Report, the survey observers grouped together to form Organisation Cetacea (ORCA), a non-profit making organisation. ORCA provides a forum for those interested in whales and dolphins by providing information, helping people throughout the region to exchange news and views on whale-watching and the latest events.

Since surveys began in 1996, at least 300 members of the public have participated in research with ORCA and an estimated 1,000 people have travelled on board the ferries specifically to watch whales and dolphins. The research work carried out by ORCA has shown that the Bay of Biscay is one of the most important regions of the world for cetaceans and that it supports a higher cetacean biodiversity than any other comparable area in the north-east Atlantic.

ORCA research has also helped to raise awareness of the threats that cetaceans face in the Bay of Biscay and elsewhere. Although whaling ceased in this part of the North Atlantic over 20 years ago, many species within the region, like other parts of the world, face other hazards. Factors which currently affect cetaceans include increased disturbance by shipping, loss of prey through over-fishing, increased levels of pollution and, perhaps, the long-term effects of global climate change. However, it is generally recognised that one of the most significant threats to cetaceans in this region, particularly dolphins and porpoises, is accidental capture or entanglement in fishing nets – so called 'by-catches'. For example, between February and March 2000 a total of 400 cetaceans, mainly Common Dolphins, stranded dead on the Atlantic coasts of France and south-west England. At least 80% of the animals examined showed signs of entanglement in fishing nets. Although 400 deaths may not represent a large proportion of the dolphin populations of the region, it has been calculated that the stranded corpses possibly represent only 10–20% of those killed and deposited at sea. Some marine scientists fear the total mortality could be far worse, and that the stranded individuals may represent just the tip of the iceberg. Further research, particularly on winter fisheries, is therefore urgently required to ascertain the extent of the 'by-catch' which is occurring in this region.

The research carried out by ORCA and other organisations on the relative abundance and distribution of cetaceans will continue to be of key importance in identifying areas of high conservation priority. At a time when this fragile ecosystem faces so many threats, ORCA is working with other research and conservation organisations including the Whale and Dolphin Conservation Society, Seawatch Foundation and the Spanish Cetacean Society to increase protection for whales and dolphins and the marine environment.

At a time when conservation and research funding is limited, the work of volunteers is becoming increasingly important in collecting data. Ship-based surveys of the Bay of Biscay and adjacent waters by volunteers, can provide marine biologists with further data which may be relevant to the formulation of cetacean conservation policies. To assist us with this research, ORCA would be very grateful to receive any (including past) records of cetacean sightings in the Bay of Biscay and the English Channel in order to incorporate them into the next report. Please send your cetacean sightings to the authors c/o ORCA.

Other correspondence relating to ORCA including membership should be sent to: Secretary, Organisation Cetacea, 9 Prospect Row, St. Neots, Cambridgeshire, PE19 1JS.

Further reading

A Field Guide to Whales, Porpoises and Seals from Cape Cod to Newfoundland. S.K. Katona, V. Rough & D.T. Richardson. 1993. Smithsonian IP, USA.

Among Whales. Roger Payne. 1996. Bantum Press, USA.

Dolphins and Whales from the Azores. S. Vialle. 1997. Portugal.

Eyewitness Handbook of Whales, Dolphins and Propoises. M. Carwardine. 1995. Dorling Kindersley, London.

Guide to the Identification of Whales, Dolphins and Porpoises in European Seas. P.G.H. Evans. 1995. Scottish Natural Heritage, U.K.

ORCA No 1. A Report on the Whales, Dolphins and Seabirds of the Bay of Biscay and the English Channel. G. Cresswell & D. Walker (eds.). 2001. Organisation Cetacea, UK.

The Bay of Biscay Cetacean Report 1997. D. Walker (ed). 1998. Organisation Cetacea, UK.

The Bay of Biscay Cetacean Report 1998. G. Cresswell & D. Walker (eds). 1999. Organisation Cetacea, UK.

The Natural History of Whales and Dolphins. P.G.H. Evans. 1987. Cambridge University Press.

The Sierra Club Handbook of Whales and Dolphins of the World. S. Leatherwood & R. Reeves. 1988. Sierra Club, USA.

Whales. P. Clapham. 1997. Colin Baxter. World Wildlife Library. UK.

Whales and Dolphins – Guide to the Biology and Behaviour of Cetaceans. M. Wuirtz & N. Repetto. 1998. Swan Hill Press.

Whales and Dolphins – The Ultimate Guide to Marine Mammals. M. Carwardine, E. Hoyt, R. Ewan Fordyce & P. Gill. 1998. Harper Collins.

Whales of the North Atlantic. Biology and Ecology. P.H. Fountaine. 1998. Editions MultiMondes, Canada.

Useful websites

European Cetacean Society . . . . http://www.inter.nl.net/users/J.W.Broekema/ecs/
Greenpeace . . . . .http://www.greenpeace.org
Hebridean Whale and Dolphin Trust . . . . .http://www.gn.apc.org/whales
International Fund for Animal Welfare . . . . .http://www.ifaw.org
International Whaling Commission . . . .http://www.ourworld.compuserve.com/homepages/iwcoffice
Marine Conservation Society . . . . .http://www.mcsuk.org
Organisation Cetacea (ORCA) . . . . .http://www.orcaweb.org
P&O Ferries . . . . .http://www.poportsmouth.com
Sea Mammal Research Unit . . . . .http://smub.st-and.ac.uk
Sea Watch Foundation .http://www.seawatchfoundation.org.uk
Shetland Marine Mammal Group . . . . .http://www.wildlife.shetland.co.uk/
Society for Marine Mammalogy . . . . .http://pegasus.cc.ucf.edu/~smm
Spanish Cetacean Society . . . . .http://www.cetaceos.com
Tethys Research Institute . . . . .http://www.tethys.org
UKCetnet . . . . .http://www.egroups.com/community/UKCetnet
Whale and Dolphin Conservation Society . . . . .http://www.wdcs.org
WhaleNet . . . . .http://whale.wheelock.edu
Whale-Watching-Web . . . . .http://www.physics.helsinki.fi/whale
World Wide Fund for Nature . . . . .http://www.panda.org

Glossary

Baleen   Comb like plates which grow from the upper jaw of some large whales. They are used to filter food from sea water.

Beak   The snout, or forward projecting jaws of a cetacean.

Blow   The visible exhalation of a whale or dolphin.

Blow-hole   The nostril(s) of a cetacean.

Blubber   The layer of insulating fat below the skin of marine mammals.

Bow-riding   Swimming in the bow pressure-wave created by moving vessels or large whales.

Breach   Leaping clear or partially clear of the surface, usually landing with a splash.

Bull   An adult male whale or dolphin.

Calf   Young cetacean which is still being nursed by its mother.

Callosity   Rough, lumpy protrusion on the head of a right whale.

Cape   Darker region on the back of some cetaceans.

Cephalopod   Member of the Class Cephalopoda, including cuttlefish, squid and octopus.

Cetacean   A marine mammal of the Order Cetacea, which includes all the whales, dolphins and porpoises.

Chevron   A pale marking, shaped like a letter V, on the back of some Fin Whales.

Cow   An adult female whale.

Delphinid   Collective term for all dolphin-like odontocetes.

Dolphin   Small cetacean which usually has a beak, conical-shaped teeth, and a falcate dorsal fin.

Dorsal   A directional term meaning towards the back or upper-side.

Dorsal fin   The upper or top fin in marine vertebrates.

Echolocation   The location of objects by reflected sound.

Falcate   Sickle-shaped and curved backwards.

Flipper   the forelimbs of marine mammals, including cetaceans, pinnipeds and manatees.

Flipper-slapping   Raising the flipper or pectoral fin out of the water and slapping it on the surface.

Flukes   The horizontally flattened tail of cetaceans that function as an organ of propulsion.

Juvenile   Young cetacean that is independent of its mother, but is not fully mature.

Krill   Small, shrimp-like crustaceans.

Lob-tailing   Raising tail flukes into the air and slapping them on the surface.

Logging   The act of lying still on or near the surface.

Lunge-feedng   Baleen whales occasionally exhibit this behaviour. Their heads lunge vertically out of the water, jaws wide open in an attempt to surprise and engulf schooling prey.

Melon   The bulbous forehead of some toothed cetaceans.

Mysticeti   The Order of baleen whales.

Odontoceti   The Order of toothed whales.

Pectoral fin   The flippers or forelimbs of a cetacean.

Pelagic   Oceanic, inhabiting the open sea; living in the surface waters or middle depths of the ocean.

Pod   A discrete, coordinated group of cetaceans.

Porpoise   Small cetacean with an indistinct beak or no beak, spade-shaped teeth, and usually a small, triangular dorsal fin.

Porpoising   Leaping clear of the water whilst swimming rapidly forwards.

Rorqual   A baleen whale of the genus *Balaenoptera*.

Rostrum   The beak or snout of a baleen whale.

Sounding-dive   Deep dive, usually following a series of shorter, shallower dives.

Splash guard   Area around the blow-hole of some whales which is raised during the breathing sequence.

Spout   A column of spray thrown into the air by a whale when breathing.

Spy-hopping   A behaviour that involves a cetacean raising its head vertically above the water surface.

Stranding   When a cetacean comes ashore, either dead or alive.

Tail-stock   The tapered rear part of the body from behind the dorsal fin to the tail flukes.

Temperate   Mid-latitude region, between the polar and sub-tropical waters, characterised by a mild climate.

Terminal dive   Deep dive, usually following a series of short, shallower dives, when flukes are most likely to be seen.

Throat grooves   Grooves or pleats in the throat region of some whales.

Transient   Group of cetaceans which move through an area as opposed to resident populations.

Tubercles   Raised knobs or lumps, such as those on the head of a Humpback Whale.

Ventral   Pertaining to the underside of the body.

Ventral pleats   The longitudinal grooves on the undersurface of some species of baleen whale.

Checklist of Species

Plate	Species	Likelihood of Observation	Number	Behaviour / notes
1	Northern Right Whale	★★★★★		
1	Blue Whale	★★★★★		
2	Sei Whale	★★★★		
2	Fin Whale	★★		
3	Humpback Whale	★★★★★		
3	Minke Whale	★★★		
4	Pygmy Sperm Whale	★★★★★		
4	Dwarf Sperm Whale	★★★★★		
5	Sperm Whale	★★★★		
6	Northern Bottle-nosed Whale	★★★★		
6	Cuvier's Beaked Whale	★★★★		
7	Sowerby's Beaked Whale	★★★★★		
7	Blainville's Beaked Whale	★★★★★		
8	True's Beaked Whale	★★★★★		
8	Gervais' Beaked Whale	★★★★★		
9	Rough-toothed Dolphin	★★★★★		
9	Bottle-nosed Dolphin	★★		
10	Common Dolphin	★		
10	Striped Dolphin	★★		
11	Atlantic White-sided Dolphin	★★★★		
11	White-beaked Dolphin	★★★★		
12	Long-finned Pilot Whale	★		
12	Short-finned Pilot Whale	★★★★★		
13	False Killer Whale	★★★★★		
13	Orca	★★★★		
14	Risso's Dolphin	★★★		
14	Harbour Porpoise	★★★		

LIKELIHOOD OF OBSERVATION: The number of stars indicates the likelihood of observing the species during a voyage across the Bay of Biscay during the species' peak abundance months. It should therefore be used in conjunction with the relative abundance bar chart and species distribution map.

★ = 90–100% certain   ★★★★★ = extremely unlikely

Photographic and Artwork Credits

Photographs by the Authors: Graeme Cresswell = (GC); Dylan Walker = (DW)

Front/back Cover.
Striped Dolphin: Porpoising; Gulf of Mexico; Dagmar C. Fertl.
Humpback Whale: Fluking; Keflavik; Iceland; June 1998; (DW).

Endpaper illustrations: Phil Coles

Frontispiece.
Orca: Shetland Islands, Scotland; Hugh Harrop.

p. 7 **Humpback Whale** and **Northern Bottle-nosed Whale**: Illustration; Rob Still.
p. 11 **Risso's Dolphin**: Chorus line (pod logging); Manado, North Sulawesi, Indonesia; September 1998; Carla Benoldi.
p. 11 **Northern Bottle-nosed Whale**: Tail-slapping; Isle of Skye, Scotland; August. 1998; (DW).
p. 11 **Blue Whale**: Blow; Snaefellsness, Iceland; June 1998; (DW).
p. 11 **Humpback Whale**: Tail; Maui, Hawaii, USA; February 1996; Lori Mazzuca.
p. 11 **Short-finned Pilot Whales**: Logging; Tenerife; September 1998; (DW).
p. 11 **Long-finned Pilot Whale**: Spy-hopping; Ligurian Sea, Italy; 1999; Robin Baird.
p. 11 **Humpback Whale**: Breaching; Maui, Hawaii, USA; March 1996; Lori Mazzuca.
p. 11 **Dusky and Common Dolphins**: Porpoising; Kaikoura, New Zealand; March 1999; Sam Taylor.
p. 12 **Whale-watchers**: Bay of Biscay; July 1997; (GC).
p. 13 **Northern Right Whale** Cape Cod; 1996; Robin Baird.
p. 13 **Blue Whale**: Olafsvik, Iceland; June 1998; (GC).
p. 14 **Sperm Whale**: Manado, North Sulawesi, Indonesia; August 1998; Pietro Pecchioni.
p. 14 **Northern Bottle-nosed Whale**: Isle of Skye, Scotland; August 1998: (DW).
p. 15 **Short-finned Pilot Whale**: Tenerife; February 1998; (DW).
p. 15 **Common Dolphin**: Porpoising; Mercury Bay, New Zealand; March 1999; Dirk Neumann.
p. 16 **Harbour Porpoise**: Bay of Fundy, Novia Scotia, Canada; January 1998; (GC).
p. 16 **Minke Whale**: Breaching; Richard Smith.

PLATE 1
Northern Right Whale: Head/head and jaw/tail flukes; three images; Cape Cod; 1996; Robin Baird.
Blue Whale: Tail flukes; California, USA; August 2000; (GC).
Blue Whale: Initial surface/head and back/Back and dorsal fin; three images, one individual; Snaefellsness, Iceland; June 1998; (DW).

PLATE 2
Sei Whale: Surfacing/Blowing; Azores; Doug Perrine/Innerspace Visions (blow; digital illustration by Rob Still).
Sei Whale: Surfacing; Azores; Doug Perrine/Innerspace Visions.
Fin Whale: Back and dorsal fin; Monterey Bay, California, USA; August 1997; (GC).
Fin Whale: Right jaw/Left jaw; two images; Gulf of St. Lawrence, Canada; August 1998; (GC).
Fin Whale: Blow-hole and blow; Bay of Fundy, Canada; August 1998; (GC).

PLATE 3
Humpback Whale: Pair surfacing; Keflavik, Iceland; June 1998; (GC).
Humpback Whale: Diving; Keflavik, Iceland; June 1998; (DW).
Humpback Whale: Tail; Maui, Hawaii, USA; February 1996; Lori Mazzuca.
Minke Whale: Back and dorsal fin; Gulf of St. Lawrence, Canada; August 1998; (GC).
Minke Whale: Head and back; Gulf of St. Lawrence, Canada; August 1998; (GC).
Minke Whale: From above; George McCallum/Whalephoto Berlin.

PLATE 4
Pygmy Sperm Whale: Digital artwork by Rob Still.
Dwarf Sperm Whale: Colin Macleod.

PLATE 5
Sperm Whale: Head, Shetland Islands, Scotland; Hugh Harrop.
Sperm Whale: Tail; Norway; George McCallum/Whalephoto Berlin.
Sperm Whale: Blow; KaiKoura, New Zealand; January 1999; Sam Taylor.
Sperm Whale: Back; Shetland Islands, Scotland; Hugh Harrop.
Beaked whales: heads; Digital artwork by Rob Still.

PLATE 6
Northern Bottle-nosed Whale: Breaching; Isle of Skye, Scotland; Aug. 1998; (DW).
Northern Bottle-nosed Whale: Tail-slapping; Isle of Skye, Scotland; August 1998; (DW).
Northern Bottle-nosed Whale: Surfacing; Isle of Skye, Scotland; August 1998; (DW).
Northern Bottle-nosed Whale: Surfacing; Isle of Skye, Scotland; August 1998; (GC).
Cuvier's Beaked Whale: Adult female; Bahamas; Colin MacLeod.
Cuvier's Beaked Whale: Dark-headed individual; Bay of Biscay, Spain; July 1997; Jonathan Mitchell.
Cuvier's Beaked Whale: Head; Hatteras, New Carolina, USA; July 2000; Bruce Hallett.

PLATE 7
Sowerby's Beaked Whale: (Top and bottom) two individuals together; Azores; Lisa Steiner/Whalewatch Azores.
Sowerby's Beaked Whale: (Centre) Back/head; two images, same individual; The Gully, Novia Scotia; July 1997; Robin Baird.
Blainville's Beaked Whale: Female; two images, same individual; Canary Islands; 1995; George McCallum/Whalephoto Berlin.
Blainville's Beaked Whale: Male; Canary Islands; 1995; George McCallum/Whalephoto Berlin.
Blainville's Beaked Whale: Female; Bahamas; Colin Macleod.

PLATE 8
True's Beaked Whale: Head, dorsal fin and back; Digital artwork by Rob Still.
?True's Beaked Whale: Back/head; two images, same individual; Azores; Lisa Steiner/Whalewatch Azores.
Gervais' Beaked Whale: Back; Tenerife; Sergio Hanquet.
Gervais' Beaked Whale: Head; Tenerife; Sergio Hanquet.

PLATE 9
Rough-toothed Dolphin: Two animals breaching; Tahiti; May 1999; Sam Taylor.
Rough-toothed Dolphin: Surfacing; 800 km west of Honduras; November 1998; Stephanie A. Norman.
Bottle-nosed Dolphin: Porpoising; Oahu, Hawaii, USA; April 1996; Lori Mazzuca.
Bottle-nosed Dolphin: Surfacing; Tenerife; October 1998; (DW).

PLATE 10
Common Dolphin: Porpoising; Mercury Bay, New Zealand; March 1999; Dirk Neumann.
Common Dolphin: Surfacing; Gibraltar; April 1999; (GC).
Common Dolphin: Two animals surfacing; Bay of Biscay, Spain; August 1999; (DW).
Striped Dolphin: Surfacing; Gibraltar; April 1999; (GC).
Striped Dolphin: Porpoising; Gulf of Mexico; Dagmar C. Fertl.
Striped Dolphin: Surfacing; Gibraltar; April 1999; (GC).

PLATE 11
Atlantic White-sided Dolphin: Two animals surfacing; The Gully, Novia Scotia; Sascha Hooker.
White-beaked Dolphin: Surfacing; Keflavik, Iceland; June 1998; (DW).
White-beaked Dolphin: Breaching; Keflavik, Iceland; June 1998; (DW).
White-beaked Dolphin: Surfacing; Keflavik, Iceland; June 1998; (DW).

PLATE 12
Long-finned Pilot Whale: Group; Ligurian Sea, Italy; 1999; Robin Baird.
Long-finned Pilot Whale: Spy-hopping; Ligurian Sea, Italy; 1999; Robin Baird.
Long-finned Pilot Whale: Mother and calf; Novia Scotia; August 1997; Robin Baird.
Short-finned Pilot Whale: Group; Tenerife; October 1998; (DW).
Short-finned Pilot Whale: Mother and calf; Tenerife; April 2000; (GC).
Short-finned Pilot Whale: Head at surface; Tenerife; November 1998; (DW).

PLATE 13
False Killer Whale: Breaching; Mercury Bay, New Zealand; January 1999; Dirk Neumann.
False Killer Whale: Surfacing; Lana'i, Hawaii, USA; April 1997; Lori Mazzuca.
Orca: Family pod; Snaefellsness, Iceland; June 1998; (GC).
Orca: Dorsal fin; Olafsvik, Iceland; June 1998; (DW).
Orca: Adult male; Kaikoura, New Zealand; January 1999; Sam Taylor.

PLATE 14
Risso's Dolphin: Chorus line (pod logging); Manado, North Sulawesi, Indonesia; September 1998; Carla Benoldi.
Risso's Dolphin: Pair surfacing; Manado, North Sulawesi, Indonesia; September 1998; Carla Benoldi.
Harbour Porpoise: Group; Bay of Fundy, Novia Scotia, Canada; January 1998; (GC).

pp. 46–47. Surfacing sequences of larger whales: illustrations by Rob Still.

p. 48. **Sunfish**: South-west Spain; (GC).

54

Index

Índice

INDEX OF ENGLISH AND SCIENTIFIC NAMES

This index includes the English and *scientific* names of all the cetaceans mentioned in the text.

Figures in *italicised bold red text* refer to the number of the plate(s) on which the species is illustrated.
Figures in *italicised bold black text* indicate the page number(s) on which there is another illustration.
Figures in **bold text** refer to the page on which the main text for the species can be found.

White-beaked Dolphin

Atlantic White-sided Dolphin

Harbour Porpoise

Common Dolphin

Striped Dolphin

False Killer Whale

Risso's Dolphin

Rough-toothed Dolphin

Bottle-nosed Dolphin